Writing Workouts to Develop Common Core Writing Skills

Writing Workouts to Develop Common Core Writing Skills

Step-by-Step Exercises, Activities, and Tips for Student Success, Grades 7–12

Kendall Haven

LIBRARIES UNLIMITED

AN IMPRINT OF ABC-CLIO, LLC
Santa Barbara, California • Denver, Colorado • Oxford, England

Library of Congress Cataloging-in-Publication Data

Haven, Kendall F.

  Writing workouts to develop Common Core writing skills : step-by-step exercises, activities, and tips for student success, grades 7–12 / Kendall Haven.

    pages cm

  Includes bibliographical references and index.

  ISBN 978–1–61069–868–9 (pbk.) — ISBN 978–1–61069–869–6 (ebook) 1. English language—Composition and exercises—Study and teaching (Secondary) I. Title.

LB1631.H295 2015

808′.0420712—dc23   2014027060

ISBN: 978–1–61069–868–9
EISBN: 978–1–61069–869–6

19 18 17 16 15   1 2 3 4 5

This book is also available on the World Wide Web as an eBook.
Visit www.abc-clio.com for details.

Libraries Unlimited
An Imprint of ABC-CLIO, LLC

ABC-CLIO, LLC
130 Cremona Drive, P.O. Box 1911
Santa Barbara, California 93116-1911

This book is printed on acid-free paper ∞

Manufactured in the United States of America

*This book is dedicated to
the students
of the Franklin Unified School District
who helped me refine and test
a number of these activities.*

CONTENTS

INTRODUCTION

Why learn to write? Writing is hard. Teaching writing devours large chunks of classroom time in every grade. Blocks of time each day are devoted to spelling, to grammar, to vocabulary, and to other mechanical aspects of writing. Precious little time can be squeezed from the remains of each day's mandates to work on teaching students how to effectively and powerfully communicate when they write. That is, to plan, draft, evaluate, revise, and edit whatever content they want to (or have been assigned to) write. It is a legitimate question to ask: why bother? Why dedicate so much time to writing?

Learning to write should never be viewed as an end goal in and of itself. Rather, writing is a means to a goal (effective communication). "Writing" doesn't mean "learn the symbols and write them down." It means "convince, persuade, inspire, entertain, and teach through your writing as effectively as you would through conversation if you and the reader sat next to each other on the sofa." This book provides a variety of tested writing activities that can guide students to that level of writing competency.

GOAL

The new Common Core standards require that students develop the ability to write beyond spelling and forming a sentence. They must translate mental images, ideas, and emotions into written language that successfully transfers those ideas, images, and emotions to another person. Beyond the mechanical skills of spelling, grammar, sentence structure, punctuation, and vocabulary lie the writing skills that allow the writer to powerfully and effectively *communicate*—ideas, concepts, images. Those are the writing skills that this book is designed to develop. You want your students to comfortably possess the writing know-how to effectively communicate whatever they want to get across on paper. This book will help.

The obvious goal of a writing book is to build basic writing skill, muscle, and confidence. However, equally important, successful writing programs develop a positive writing attitude in students. Teachers and librarians need to build writing *enthusiasm* as well as writing ability.

Without a modicum of enthusiasm for writing, any skill improvement will quickly atrophy from lack of use and practice.

That writing is an important skill is not debated or questioned. Research also shows that mastery of writing process links to general education success and to students' analytical, logical, and general mental development. After several years of study, the College Board test creators released the following statement in mid-2010: "Of all the sections of the SAT, the writing section is the most predictive of college success." Through two earlier studies of my own, I have been able to establish a direct, positive link between writing skill development and improved reading comprehension. Learning to effectively write seems to be a "gateway" precursor to mastery of other academic subjects or skill sets.

Reasonably-rapid, effective writing is a basic 21st-century life skill, as well as an academic skill of increasing importance under the demands of the common core standards and standardized testing. One goal of this book is to provide writing activities that help each teacher squeeze as much writing proficiency development out of each available minute as possible. Once developed, these core writing skills allow students to readily respond to a variety of prompts and writing response styles. This book will arm librarians and teachers with tools, proven activities, and research-based concepts that will allow them to better guide their students toward successful writing proficiency.

WHAT MAKES WRITING HARD?

If writing is so important to students' general development, why, then, is it consistently so hard for students to master writing? Why is writing so much harder than talking? Setting aside the mechanical challenges of writing (holding a pen, placing fingers on a keyboard, having thumbs blur across a cell phone keypad), the wiring and structure of the human brain hold important evolutionary answers.

Humans have been speaking for over 1,000,000 years. We can document that they were telling stories to each other several hundred thousand years ago. Because of this long dependence on speech, the human brain now has dedicated regions (especially Broca's and Wrenicke's areas and those sub-regions surrounding the Sylvian fissure) dedicated to processing language and speech. Children learn to speak all on their own because their brains are wired to emphasize and to develop that ability.

Not so with writing and reading. Writing (like reading) is a new human activity. Sumerian—generally agreed to be the first written language—is no more than 7,000 years old. At the time of the American Revolution, far less than half of the American population was literate. In the long history of humanoids on this planet, we have been reading and writing *en masse* for only the tiniest fraction of time.

There is no brain center for writing. Our DNA carries no genes for writing or reading. There may be in another 100,000 years. But not now. Lacking any dedicated brain space, learning to read and write must steal space from other brain areas as those processes are taught and learned.

Speaking is naturally and automatically learned by each individual. Writing, like reading, is not.

The tools and activity of writing must be systematically taught. It requires engaging activities that stretch skills while holding the attention and focus of students. Enter this book with its series of powerful and proven tips and writing activities. I have crafted these workout activities by combining my in-class experience in over 3,000 schools and over 12,000 individual classrooms (the practical what-*really*-works? experience) with extensive research into story structure and the cognitive effects of individual story elements to produce the activities included here.

I have in-class tested each of these activities multiple times in multiple schools in multiple states—many used over 100 times at each of the recommended grade levels. These work. They are time efficient. They develop the essential writing muscle to apply to a variety of writing tasks and prompts listed on standardized writing assignments in virtually every state.

Writing skills can be broken into two distinct groups of skills that are typically presented in separate blocks—or periods—of instruction in American schools.

- **Mechanical skills:** spelling, grammar, sentence structure, punctuation, capitalization, and vocabulary
- **Content skills:** planning, researching, drafting, evaluating, revising, and editing the material to be written

This book focuses primarily on the ***content*** aspects of writing since virtually every school language arts textbook focuses primarily (and often almost exclusively) on the mechanical aspects of writing. I will touch on mechanical concerns only in the section on editing.

PREVIOUS WRITING BOOKS

Available research conclusively shows that story structure underlies successful formation of the "thing" to be communicated if that "thing" is to be compelling and effective. That notion was the basis for my book *Story Proof* and my new follow-on book, *Story Smart*. Those books focus not on the process of communicating something to an audience or reader, but on how to organize and structure the information you want to communicate—and on the neural and cognitive science that explains the power and effectiveness of what we commonly call "effective story structure." Those two books do not deal directly with the act of communicating, but with creating and planning the structural architecture to later be communicated.

Story Proof and *Story Smart* collectively provide the research basis for centering the planning and development process around the Eight Essential Elements of effective story structure. My Libraries Unlimited books *Get It Write!* and *Write Right!* provide (combined) over 100 games and activities to teach that structure and those informational elements to students. Collectively, those books address the writer's planning process. That is, they guide students into the habit of planning and creating effective material to communicate before they begin to actually write (or speak).

Get It Write! is about exercising individual elements of effective story structure (like practicing individual instruments of an orchestra). This book is about writing flowing music for the orchestra as a whole once you know what the individual instruments each can do to contribute to the overall musical sound you want to create. To do that, we will focus on honing the skills of writing in conjunction with the skills of creating.

USING THIS BOOK

All TIPs and workouts of the book link to core curriculum elements and to state language arts standards for virtually every state. However, this book is not designed to serve as a formal language arts textbook. Rather, it will serve as a comprehensive, proven guide with in-class tested activities to arm teachers and school librarians with the approaches, knowledge, and activities to meet their students' needs and to teach and inspire their students to write.

I have collected solid research-based underpinnings for all concepts and techniques to be included. However, I do not intend to focus on a presentation of research. Rather, I will focus on the practical application of tested research concepts. I have personally, and repeatedly, tested every activity to be included in the book and will rely heavily on that personal in-class experience and results in presenting detailed directions for the use of these materials.

I have designed the assignments to be fun as well as instructive—fun both for teacher and for students. I have successfully used every activity I include, and have gotten positive teacher and student feedback on each. The range of included activities will make students **want** to write. Only then can teachers effectively teach them **how** to write.

The book is also conceived to work within the realities of modern schools and classrooms. This will be a practical guide that will efficiently—as well as effectively—improve student writing performance within the fierce constraints and realities under which librarians and teachers must function.

I regularly include time for review and discussion in most of the workouts. I have seen great value in classroom after classroom from seeing/hearing what other students did with the same assignment. These interludes also provide time for reflection and mental revision, a chance for students to ponder their own writing efforts and successes. I believe that these sharing and review periods are amazingly important to the advancement of all but your very top students.

Is there any significance to the order of individual workouts? Answer: no. Feel free to jump around and use those that fit with the flow of your classroom teaching. Every workout in this book has consistently created both writing enthusiasm and significantly improved writing skill. Enjoy!

CHAPTER 1

THE WRITER'S TOOLBOX

Every carpenter drags a personal box of tools to each jobsite. That toolbox contains all of the essential tools and supplies the carpenter needs in order to get the assigned job done. But that carpenter also drags a mental toolbox to the jobsite that contains his/her accumulated knowledge of how to effectively use each tool.

Similarly, each writer is armed with both a physical and a mental writing toolbox that he hauls around to each writing assignment. While the writer's physical toolbox (vocabulary, spelling, grammar, punctuation, penmanship, etc.) is both real and important, it is his mental toolbox—his experience of writing concepts and techniques that will allow him to combine, mold, maneuver, and manipulate words to successfully communicate—that is most important and also the focus of this book.

How does a writer create suspense and excitement? Or create and develop interesting characters? Or build the tension around a climax? Or grab readers with an opening hook? Or create consistently vivid and compelling imagery? Or build a convincing and persuasive case for her ideas? Or draw readers into a story so that they vicariously experience the story events? These are some of the writing tools student writers can develop through these workouts and tuck away in their mental writer's toolbox.

THE FIVE STEPS OF SUCCESSFUL WRITING

Ask your class, "What makes a good writer?" and let them discuss and develop their collective answer. I have asked this question of many students, but also of groups of professional storytellers and story writers.

Many answer that "some have the gift, and most of us don't." That is—in my opinion—both wrong and overly simplistic. Certainly, natural writing ability is distributed among us humans on a normal distribution curve. (You know that classic distribution curve—technically a Poisson distribution—that tapers off smoothly and evenly at both ends and with a great hump in the middle.) Running ability, artistic talent, singing, cooking, fiddle playing, mechanical drawing, and every other specific skill seems to be distributed according to the same pattern. Some naturally are given greater writing ability. True enough. But that begs the question: what makes a good writer? That is, can *any* student, starting with whatever natural writing talent she possesses, become a sufficiently "good" writer to be consistently *effective* in her writing? And what does it take for her to do so?

That's the real question. After much observation and thought, here is my six-part answer.

1. Be curious, observe. Probe. Pose questions. Explore. Be easily fascinated. Peer beyond the surface of things, people, and ideas. Treat everything as if it were a mechanical clock begging to be disassembled—just so you can see how it works.

2. Master story structure. (The Eight Essential Elements. See TIP #5.) These eight elements reflect how the reader's brain is hardwired to make sense out of what he or she reads. Master those eight elements and you make it easy for readers to understand and make sense from what you write. I have written several books on these elements and the process of using them.

3. Read—often and critically. Enjoy reading. But also critically analyze what the writer did—both when you enjoyed the writing and when you didn't. How did they get you to see images of their story? How did they get you to feel different emotions? How did they structure their sentences and paragraphs? Etc.

4. Write. The more you do it, the better you get. Also, critically evaluate your own writing. Don't beat yourself up, but honestly decide what worked as you hoped it would and how you would write it differently next time.

5. Always be willing to revise and edit. ("I *will* remember the 1st rule of writing: No one gets it right on the 1st draft." See TIP #2.)

6. Master the mechanics of writing. These are the technical tools of the trade. Every painter needs to master brushstrokes. Every dancer spends hours holding onto a bar practicing basic positions and single moves. These are the fundamental tools artists use to express themselves. And, yes, writing is an art; and, yes, you need to master those basic mechanical tools of writing.

That said, effective writing isn't a single process. In fact, it is the end result of five separate steps, each with its own concerns, goals, focus, pace, and techniques. In order to produce a final well-written product, the writer must plan, draft, evaluate, revise, and edit.

Step 1. Plan

Planning is all about . . . well, planning. It is the step when you take the time to create and to explore. Let your imagination soar. Use what-ifs. Think about each of the Eight Essential Elements. Try on different ideas like you'd try on different clothes at the store before you bought any.

Create first; write second. (See TIP #1.) That is the first rule of writing; the research is quite clear on this. Anyone for whom the mechanical act of writing is a conscious effort—i.e., virtually all students—can't successfully create and write at the same time. That part of the brain responsible for the mechanical acts of writing (holding pencil, fingers on keyboard, forming letters, picking the right letters, forming a sentence, etc.) has the ability to shut down the creative part of the brain. The reverse is not true. When they try to do both together (as virtually all students do), creativity falters. What is created tends to be bland, simple, plot-driven, and . . . well, boring.

Create first, and only write once the thing you create is worth writing. Talk it, talk about it, draw it, act it, doodle it. *Play* with what you are going to write, and then write. If, on timed writing assessments, students allotted 20 percent of their available time to this planning process, they would make the actual writing both far easier and far more coherent and effective.

My previous writing books, *Get It Write!* and *Write Right!*, also focus on this planning process and on developing the tools and habits that make for effective writers.

In this book I will extend the process to the development of more comprehensive tools for each student writer's toolbox—techniques to master and to (yes!) enjoy.

Step 2. Draft

Planning is when the writer builds up a reservoir of ideas and details—like piling water into a lake behind a dam. Drafting is the time to throw open the floodgates. Let the pent-up ideas gush out. This is the time to let the words fly. Write with abandon, with passion, with emotion! Drafting is the time for a "data dump," from mind to paper, a time to get all of your thoughts down on paper for the first time. Drafting is a time for letting the vivid details and emotions flow. Go for the conflict. Make it exciting! If you don't do those things during drafting, they are ever-so-much harder to install later.

Don't stop to edit, to spell check, to worry about grammar or capitalization, or to correct wording. There will be plenty of time for those activities later. During draft writing, keep writing. No, there is no need to draft an entire story, article, or report all at once. Break it into logical chunks (section, chapter, scene), and draft those individually once you are ready with the images and details for that part of the whole. Then stop and prep for the next part you'll draft. Put it together and smooth it out after you have written each individual part.

Don't worry if you don't know exactly where to begin. First-draft beginnings are always wrong and need to be changed and revised later. So don't worry about it. Dive in and start, knowing full well that it will be easy to fix it once you see the entire story on paper.

First drafts are always lousy. Still, they are a critically important step in the process. Plan as best you can. Then trust yourself and write! No, not all experienced writers write this way. But it is my experience in working with students that it is by far the best writing plan for beginning writers.

Step 3. Evaluate

Evaluation is that step most teachers and students overlook. It's the step there is never enough time to formally include in student writing efforts. Evaluation is that step wherein a writer decides exactly what needs to be revised and edited—and what does not. Often, after formal evaluation, small and simple changes can make huge—and extremely satisfying—improvements in the success of the piece.

Far too many student writers, however, finish drafting and instantly dive into editing. Don't do it. Write it and set it aside. Then come back and evaluate the writing. What works? Where do you need to add paragraphs or scenes? Where do you need to cut? Are the characters interesting and well developed? Are the Eight Elements all there? Did you begin at the best spot? Does each scene have sufficient details? Are the opening, climax, and resolution all satisfying? Will the reader easily follow the flow of the main character's struggles?

I included a large section on evaluation in my book *Write Right!* and refer you to that book for detailed ideas for both self-evaluation and peer-evaluation techniques.

It is immensely difficult for writers to evaluate their own writing. Why? They already know exactly what they wanted to say. They already hold detailed images of each scene and point in their minds. Thus, *any* words on the page will pop those already-existing images back into their head—and those images are perfect! Many student writers conclude that, therefore, the words they wrote must also be perfect—or at least completely adequate.

A writer cannot accurately evaluate what they write until all of the images have dissipated that they formed in their mind in order to write. Research says that, for most people, that takes several weeks. However, classrooms rarely afford that time luxury. The alternative is to provide a structured process—an evaluation checklist—for students to use either for author evaluations or for peer evaluations.

Remember: you can't fix it until you decide exactly what needs to be fixed. If you have a leak in a plumbing system, you don't attack the problem by randomly changing pieces of pipe. No. First you evaluate. You find out exactly what leaks and only change out those parts. Same with writing.

First drafts are always lousy. Good writers always take the time to make them better. That begins not with revision and editing, but with evaluation.

Do you have to take the time for this step on every student writing effort? Absolutely not. However, students should include it often enough to understand *how* to evaluate their writing, what evaluation does for their writing, and the impact on the quality of their final written product when there isn't sufficient time for this step.

Step 4. Revise

"Revise" and "edit" are separate steps. Every teacher wants students to edit. Every student knows about (and usually loathes) editing. No one pays much attention to revision. It, like evaluation, is an often overlooked step that can fix many problems with a draft that editing cannot touch.

Publishers often call editing "line editing" because you go over every line, and every word. Not so during revision. Here we play with big hunks of the story: move scenes, add scenes, reorder the scenes, build tension through the first half of the story, decide if the climax works or if you need to build that scene, rewrite the opening to better hook and grab readers, revise the character description for one character that you have sprinkled throughout the story so that readers get a stronger emotional reaction to him/her, sprinkle more humor throughout . . . that sort of thing.

It is important to revise *before* editing. Why? Because I have observed that, once students struggle to find just the right adjective for one sentence, or just the right bit of sensory detail, then they will never—NEVER—be willing to cut it, even if they later decide that that entire paragraph should go. They would much prefer to leave that precious detail in, even if it kills the story and ruins their grade.

While revising, a writer will often chop out multiple paragraphs and decide to completely rewrite others. Anyone already committed to a sprinkling of precious details will never be willing to do the hard work of sending them to the trash heap. (In writing circles, it's called "Kill Your Darlings.")

Often, the only way to build in time (especially your time as well as student writing time) for a real couple of rounds of revision is to do it on things students write for core curriculum subjects (reports on the stars, on explorers, on social studies topics, etc.).

Step 5. Edit

Editing is all about precision, the process of making sure that every word, phrase, sentence, and paragraph conveys exactly what you intended for them to convey. Once the story is set in place, it's time to focus on the details, on individual words. Editing is the great time sink of writing. By most estimates, easily 90 percent of the time professional writers spend writing, they spend editing. Editing is like polishing. You can't polish your way to a great marble statue. The statue has to be carved, shaped, and molded in the previous steps. Polishing then brings out its greatest glowing luster. Polishing makes the piece look as luminous and breathtaking as possible. Wood-carvers and stonemasons never actually finish polishing. They just keep at it until the piece is taken away.

Same with writing.

Writers examine every sentence, phrase, word, and detail—and the images they create. Can I find a better word that is more interesting, more descriptive, more powerful, more efficient, more unusual, more "grabbing"? Start to finish. Top to bottom. Then you start over and do it again, searching for yet better words, descriptions, and images.

Once the words are set, then, on one last edit run-through, check spelling. No need to check spelling until you're sure you are going to keep the words you check.

There are many decent guides to editing for students. I included a detailed section on it in my book *Write Right* and refer you to that book for editing checklists and progressions.

DO YOU HAVE TO DO THEM ALL?

Teachers are forever pressed for time. Many express the frustration that they don't even have adequate time to teach minimal proficiency in the mechanical skills of writing, and certainly don't have time (either their own out-of-class time or student in-class time) to extend each writing project through extensive planning, evaluation, revision, and editing.

The questions arise: if I can't do them all, is there any point in doing anything beyond a single student draft with quick mechanical editing correction? Which of the other steps are the most important? The least important? If I don't have very much time, which step(s) will prove most productive?

Here is my advice. Each of those steps is a valuable—even necessary—part of an effective writing package. However, that doesn't mean that you must include time for them all on every writing activity. For each student writing effort, decide what you want your students to focus on for that particular bit of writing.

If, for example, you opt to skip evaluation and revision, and to limit editing to one quick pass to correct mechanical errors (spelling, grammar, and capitalization), that's fine. However, you should tell students the steps you expect them to do and which they (for this assignment) should skip. That places this writing within the greater context of the complete writing process. I recommend that you also briefly discuss with students how those omitted steps are likely to impact the quality of their final product.

Having said that, I also believe that emerging student writers gain more from an emphasis on different steps at different grade levels. I would assign the steps (other than drafting—something that is always done) in this order of importance for student writing development.

1. **Planning.** Effective pre-writing planning is the most productive habit students can develop. It applies to the writing at all grade levels form first grade through graduate school.

   Without a bit of time devoted just to planning, there is little point in seriously going further. Planning doesn't require great amounts of time. A good guideline is to set aside 20 percent of total available time for planning. (Certainly, the ideal percentage will vary from student to student.) Don't worry that planning time will significantly cut into either the quantity or the quality of what students write on timed assessments. Most students find that in the remaining 80 percent they get more written, and that that writing is far better, than they would have if they had begun to write immediately.

2. **Evaluation.** Even if students do no revision or editing, it is extremely valuable to thoughtfully evaluate each piece of writing. That's how they learn. That's how they improve. I find that developing evaluation skills becomes relevant and productive beginning with the intermediate grades and develops in sophistication and depth up through high school.

3. **Revision.** Revision is an amazingly powerful and effective writing tool. At some point, every writer must grit his or her teeth and learn to do it. Revision, as a writing skill, becomes both important and manageable as students approach high school–level writing. By that time, student writing skills should have advanced to a point where they can both understand the need for specific revisions to what they write and envision the effect of possible revision schemes.

4. **Editing.** Basic editing is the one post-drafting skill drummed into every student in elementary school. That is not to say that all students are proficient and skilled as editors by the time they reach 8th or 9th grades. Learning how to quickly and efficiently manipulate words, images, and sentences in order to effectively communicate is a critical life skill. Everyone needs to be able to do it. I rank it last on this list not because students should slack off on their editing efforts by high school. Just the opposite! I list editing here because it is a more familiar part of writing for students in these grades. It is not a new set of skills to learn.

CHAPTER 2

WRITING TIPS

I visit classrooms and work with students and teachers all across the country. And I notice people driving into the same writing potholes and detouring down the same dead ends everywhere. Time after time, I notice that students stumble in the same writing spots and because of the same misconceptions.

I have distilled a "baker's dozen" writing road signs designed to help you and your students avoid those pesky writing traps into a series of TIPS. They will serve you and your students well. Recite them; chant them; write them on the wall. It would be wonderful if all 13 tips popped into students' minds whenever they think of writing.

TIP #1. CREATE FIRST; WRITE SECOND.

Research has shown that few can create and write at the same time. This is especially true for those for whom the mechanical act of writing (holding a pencil, forming letters, spelling, fluency, grammar, etc.) is at all a conscious effort. This probably includes virtually all of your students. When they try to do both together (write as they create the content they will write), they stop creating. Their content is typically uninspired, plodding, and . . . well . . . boring.

How to get around this deadly dilemma? Create first; write second. That is, don't start actually writing a narrative text until it has been planned and developed.

Try this quick demo if you doubt how deeply ingrained this write-right-away habit is. Tell your students to take out a piece of paper and get a sharpened pencil. Tell them they will have five minutes to write. Then give them a topic like "What this school needs most," or "If I ran the school," or "The class field trip I'd most like for us to take." That sort of personal opinion essay topic.

Then say "Go!" (or "Begin.") and carefully watch. My experience is that 9 out of 10 students will immediately begin to write. Most of that final 10th never get around to writing anything unless you stand glaring over their shoulder. The point is, almost all of your students just did the one thing that best guarantees lack of success in their writing. They began to write, hoping that something worth writing would appear while they wrote. Unfortunately, more often than not, it won't.

When you plan, create the Eight Essential Elements that define an effective story (see my other writing books or TIP #5, below). When planning, draw it, talk it, act it, doodle it, even jot down a few notes and key words. These activities don't impede the creative process. Writing *does*. I have developed and described dozens of prewriting activities to help students find and develop their story before they begin the first draft.

Students counter that they are terrified that they'll forget what they create if they don't write it down as they create it. I have tested this notion in hundreds of classrooms. In almost all cases, what they actually do forget was worth forgetting. What's worth remembering, they will remember if they create strong, vivid images for it as they create and plan and talk through the piece they want to write. The best solution for this "I'll forget" fear is a tape recorder. (See TIP #6.)

Then when you write, focus on the details—on selecting strong action verbs, on including powerful descriptive language.

I have also often heard that students feel squeezed for time on timed writing assessments and fear that if they don't start writing right away, they'll never finish. I have tested this notion as well. If students take the time to plan, they then write faster and more succinctly. They will actually finish in less time—and the quality of their writing will rise significantly.

Best rule of thumb: allow 20 percent of available time for planning, 80 percent for writing. Create first; write second.

TIP #2. FIRST DRAFTS ARE ALWAYS LOUSY.

No one gets it right the first time. No one. Every successful writer must revise and edit. Some very-successful writers rewrite each page as many as 50 times! If your students write mediocre—even lousy—first drafts, don't (D-O—N-O-T) allow them to think that this means they are lousy writers. It just means that they are just like everybody else: they write mediocre to lousy first drafts.

First drafts are just that . . . first drafts. Writing is rewriting. First drafts represent the process of dumping all of your thoughts down on paper for the first time. If you have planned well (pre-drafting creative activities), that first draft will be much more coherent and will flow better. But it will still be just a first draft and will still need serious revision, editing, and polishing if it is to shine with its greatest potential.

Many students claim to write perfectly acceptable—even "good"—first drafts (and thereby claim that their writing disproves this important tip). I always respond that even a *seemingly* good first draft pales in comparison to how wonderful the writing will be after several rounds of revision and editing. No one ever wrote anything near to as-good-as-it-can-be on the first draft.

Since first drafts are always lousy, have students plan on giving themselves room to revise when they draft. Double (or even triple) space all draft writing. Even better, **don't** write the first two or three drafts. Record them orally and only write the story once the student has recorded a reasonably acceptable oral draft. (See TIP #6.)

Remember, writing is not the goal, the actual product. The story (or other narrative) is. Writing is only the chosen media to communicate the actual product. Don't ever allow the media to interfere with creation and development of the actual product!

TIP #3. DON'T STOP WRITING ON THE FIRST DRAFT TO CHECK SPELLING OR GRAMMAR.

First drafts are all about passion (emotion and energy). Prewriting (before the first draft) is about planning. Postdrafting (evaluation, revision, and editing) is about precision. That wonderful first draft is the time for writers to *feel* the emotion of their story and to let their passions flow. Let your emotions out as you sling words at the page. Don't worry about the sentences, word choices, details, or spelling. Those are tasks for postdrafting. Worry about the energy, emotion, and passion of each scene.

Stopping to revise, to edit, even for a quick spell check always brings with it the unintended consequence of flattening the writing, making it dull and listless. If the fun, energy, and excitement aren't driven into the writing during that exuberant fling that we call drafting, it is extremely difficult to create them later.

If you aren't sure of the spelling, circle the word to check later and *keep writing*! If you aren't sure how to word the next sentence, skip it, leave several blank lines, and go on with what you can clearly see in your head. The idea of drafting is to let what you do know and what you can clearly see flow onto paper.

Certainly, no writer sits and drafts an entire novel, report, article, essay, or story in one sitting, in one great gush of writing. It is most common to break the whole into manageable chunks (scenes, sections, chapters, etc.) and to draft one, stop, and regroup before diving into the draft of the next chunk. It is also common to draft these chunks out of order. Start with the parts that are clearest and most vivid in your mind and draft those first. Draft each part only when you are ready, armed with vivid and detailed imagery and a strong sense of the flow and emotion of that part.

When you do, then, draft each part, don't stop to revise or rethink the writing. Focus on the characters, their emotions, and on the sensory details you would notice if you were really there—and write!

Later you can evaluate, revise, and edit to make the writing say exactly what you want it to say. It is so much easier for student writers, however, to separate these steps. Plan first, draft second, and do the grinding work of revision and editing later.

TIP #4. ON ASSESSMENT ESSAYS, *DON'T* ANSWER THE QUESTION.

WHAT? Isn't the whole point to answer the question? No. It isn't. The point is to assess—to grade—your ability to write. They want to see you write, not provide a simple answer. Honestly, no grader will fact check your essay and mark you down for getting a date wrong. They won't mark you down if the experiences you describe in your writing don't measure up to the expectations of the grader. However, they will mark you way down if your description of those experiences doesn't measure up to the expectation of the grader. They care about your writing.

If students start by answering the topical question, they often become instantly stuck, not knowing where to go or what to do next.

If the essay prompt was, for example, *tell about a time you were scared*, a legitimate answer would be "Yesterday a car honked right behind me." That's an answer—an accurate and truthful answer. But it is not what they asked for. What they really asked is "Using 'tell about a time you were scared' as a general topic and launching point, show us how well you can write!"

There is no "right answer" to those writing essay questions, anyway. Think of the prompt as a springboard to launch your writing. Think first about how you'll take advantage of this springboard to make it as easy as possible for you to write a strong, effective essay. Treat the prompt as a seed that starts your planning process. Plan what you'll specifically write about, and how you'll write about it so that you can show off the best of your writing ability and your understanding of effective story structure.

TIP #5. EFFECTIVE NARRATIVES ARE WRITTEN AROUND THE EIGHT ESSENTIAL ELEMENTS.

Here's the tip: develop the habit of planning *all* writing around the Eight Essential Elements. Two questions pop up: 1. Why? 2. What are they?

Here's the "why." The human brain is hardwired to make sense out of new information in specific story terms—the Eight Essential Elements. Extensive research and numerous studies have confirmed this statement. It's not that all readers **can** do it. It is that they automatically, without exception, *will* do it. If you develop the habit of planning for those same specific bits of information that the reader's mind requires, you will consistently deliver that key information to readers and they will be able to understand, make sense of, and become engaged by your writing.

So, what are those Eight Essential Elements? I have written several entire books on them. Here in briefest summary form:

1. **The Central Characters** who populate the key character positions in the story. *{Who am I writing about?}*

2. **The Character Traits** that make these characters interesting (memorable) to readers. *{What makes that character interesting?}*

3. **Goal**—what central characters want/need to do or get in this story. *{What do they need or want to do or get in this story?}*

4. **Motive**—why each of those goals is critically important to the character. *{Why is that goal so important?}*

5. **Problems & Conflicts** that block a character from reaching their goal. (The story's antagonist is the embodiment of the biggest of these conflicts.) *{What problems & conflicts keep the character from reaching his or her goal?}*

6. **Risk and Danger**—(the probability of failure and what happens if a character fails) created by the problems and conflicts for the main character. *{How do those problems & conflicts create risk and danger for the main character?}*

7. **Struggles**—what the character *does* (the action, the plot) to get past problems & conflicts, facing risk & danger, to get to the goal. *{What does the character do to get past problems and reach his or her goal?}*

8. **The Details** (sensory, character, scenic, action) that create mental pictures and make the story seem vivid and real. *{What details will create the key pictures in readers' minds to make the story seem real?}*

Those simple informational elements form the core structure of all successful stories and other narratives. It is actually a simple habit to develop. It also makes the process of creating narrative material easier by breaking "create your story" into smaller and easily manageable chunks. The resulting narrative is far more consistently effective.

TIP #6. TALK THE FIRST THREE DRAFTS.

Here are three well-researched and well-documented reasons to talk the initial drafts of any writing.

1. Student oral vocabulary is typically far greater than is their writing vocabulary.

2. Their willingness to include detail orally is far greater than their willingness to take the time to include that same detail in their writing.

3. Every time they say (describe) a scene, event, character, or place, they automatically build a more specific, detailed image of that thing in their minds. Then they will have more detail, clear and more specific detail, and more vivid detail in their minds when they finally do write. Say their story out loud, talk about the story, talk about the characters, sketch characters and scenes, doodle it, act it out. All of these add new mental detail. We *plan* stories, but we *write* details!

How are students to orally talk the initial drafts and not forget what they have said? Simple. Use a tape recorder (actually, any voice recording device from their smartphone, video recorder, down to an old-fashioned tape recorder). They can say it, listen to it, and mentally edit their story three times faster than they can write it once. They can also video record themselves talking their way through the first several drafts in order to capture the gestures and facial expressions that might suggest extra important detail to include when they write.

When they finally do write, they don't have to hold the story in their minds. It's on tape. Now they can focus on each sentence and on strong action verbs and on including the details.

Logistically simpler alternatives to managing how students will record and listen to their stories exist that are almost as effective. A number of effective games (especially ones like *One-On-One-On-One-On-One* (Workout #20), *The Scene Game* (Workout #29), and *The Detail Game*, described in detail in my book *Write Right!*) have been created specifically for this purpose.

TIP #7. THINK SMALL, NOT BIG, WHEN PLANNING.

I find that students tend to think of grand and epic stories—the sort of thing skilled novelists need 500 pages in order to tell. Students can't seem to stay away from grand, sweeping epics, from stories that would be difficult to stuff into a 130-minute movie, from the BIG story idea. They want to write stories of saving the world (or of conquering it). They feel compelled to include life-and-death struggles that roam across whole continents as they confront and destroy ultimate evil in every story.

Don't do it. They will never be able to write those stories. As a result, they write condensed summary overview versions—sure death by boredom to the reader.

The solution: think small (in terms of space, time, topic {goal}, and characters). By "small," I really mean *tiny*. Don't plan a story about a noble superhero knight who must raise an army to invade the vast fortress of the evil sorcerer and restore peace and freedom to the land. No. Far better to write a story about that knight picking out just the right pair of boots to wear for that invasion—and to focus on that one decision and that one moment exclusively. There is still plenty of room to develop conflict and struggle and to bring out character personalities and relationships. In fact, it is much easier to develop the essential aspects of story in small-scale stories than in grand epics.

Don't write about a person's whole life, or about a whole year. Write about one day in their life—or better yet, just a part of one day, or just one hour of a day. That's manageable. They can hold that whole story in their heads and still have a bit of mental room for creating and holding the details. In fact, once the focus of their story shrinks to this miniature size, they will be both forced and free to focus on the internal and external details that mark successful and effective writing.

Scaling stories don to a small and manageable level will let students focus on the all-important character details, sensory details, character thought processes (use TFSS; see TIP #8.), and to build each of the Eight Essential Elements. Effective writing is about the small, moment-to-moment details that build to that big picture they so eagerly lust after.

TIP #8. REMEMBER "THURSDAY, FRIDAY, SATURDAY, SUNDAY" TO BRING CHARACTERS TO LIFE.

Students naturally (and most unfortunately) focus their writing on the action—on *what* each character does. Here's the problem: the action doesn't create excitement. It doesn't make readers understand a story. It (alone) doesn't engage readers. It (by itself) won't make readers care about the story characters. It's your story *characters* that readers need to care about, not their actions. That is, readers will only value and care about story actions and events to the extent that those events explain and illuminate characters and their struggles to reach important goals.

How does a student writer induce readers to become engaged by, entranced by, and personally involved with their story characters? Actually, it's easy.

How? Readers need to know how characters think, perceive, feel, and express themselves, as well as what they actually, physically, do. That's true for every scene and for every story event.

Here is a simple mnemonic to help students remember to provide that character-based information in each story scene that readers need in order to be fully engaged by those characters and those scenes. It's the last four days of the week (if you begin the week on Monday).

Thursday, **F**riday, **S**aturday, **S**unday: T F S S. **T**hink, **F**eel, **S**ense, **S**ay. When writing each scene and each event, consider (and tell readers) what the principal characters are thinking and feeling; how they sense and perceive the scene around them; and what they say—all before you tell us what they *do* (the action).

No writer gives readers all of this information at and for every event. But every writer should picture each of theses TFSS pieces for every event and decide what readers will need (or want) to know.

With a bit of practice and some gaming, TFSS can become both automatic and an immensely powerful asset for student writing.

TIP #9. BE PICKY SHOPPERS!

You head out to shop for new clothes. Do you settle for the first items you grab as you enter a store? No. You shop! You go to your favorite stores. But you're willing to check out new ones as well. You poke through all of the racks. You compare. You try it on and see if you can use it, if it fits, if you really like it, if this is the best buy. You check out four or five stores. You get picky. And that makes for smart, successful purchases.

Be just as picky when shopping online for research information. Don't mindlessly grab the first five websites that come up on your search. Be skeptical. Be critical—just as you are when you clothes shop. Make each source convince you to use it. How reliable is this source? Do the information and the writing make sense? Where did this source get the information it presents? Do I trust those sources? Does this information fit with what I already know? Will this info be useful to me?

You'll find that you develop your favorite sites—those that consistently deliver reliable information that meets your needs (just as you develop a list of favorite clothes stores). Still, for any given information search, be willing to check out other sources. But be as skeptical when you do as you would when you check out a previously unknown clothes shop.

If you later find a flaw (an error, a misstatement), return it, as you would a shirt with missing buttonholes, and move on to other sources of information.

There are almost countless sources of information available through the Internet. Most—but certainly not all—are reliable and factual. Remember, anyone (from four-year-olds on up) can post anything on the web and claim that it is true and factual. Your job is to be a picky consumer and only use the good ones.

Just as a blouse whose seam splits wide open on the first wearing ruins your whole outfit, using one error-filled source can ruin your whole paper.

TIP #10. STRONG OPENING SENTENCES COME LAST, NOT FIRST.

Everyone wants to open with a great "grabber." Every writer wants to hook readers from the very first sentence. Two problems:

1. You can waste a whole lot of your available writing time searching for a great opening hook—and never find it—and never get your paper written.

2. You can't find the best *opening* for your story until you see exactly how your story *ends*!

Effective openings have three jobs.

1. Launch readers into the events of this story.

2. Hook the reader with some combination of character-based suspense and excitement.

3. Set up the ending, the resolution of the story.

What does this mean? Accept that you won't come up with a great opening on the first draft. If you happen to, that's great! But you are far better off assuming that you won't.

What do you do? Write the first draft starting where you think you'll begin. But don't even try to get the opening right at this point. Just start writing and get into the story (or essay, or report). Once you have finished that first draft, and once you have decided that you like the way you end your story, *then* go back and rewrite the beginning.

You'll find that it is suddenly much easier to think of, and to write, that wondrous opening hook you hoped for.

Here is one final reason not to be overly concerned with the wording of your opening hook during your first draft writing. Most of the time we start stories in the wrong place. However, you'll never notice that until after you have finished the entire first draft. Typically, we find that we can cut out the first few paragraphs—or scenes, or chapters—and be left with a much stronger "grabber" of an opening spot.

Openings are important. It is always worth spending time and effort to create the best opening you can. But the best time to do that is not when you first begin to write. It is after you have finished the whole story.

TIP #11. THREE QUESTIONS FOR BEFORE YOU WRITE ANY ESSAY.

Many students struggle to write essays. (Essays differ from articles in that essays call for the writer to make personal assessments and comments and to inject personal opinion whereas articles tend to rely on factual analysis and observation.) As a result, many students simply throw themselves at essay writing, blurting out their opinions without developing their case in a logical way and without providing the evidence that could sway the reader to agree with the writer's opinion.

One great way to avoid this essay calamity is to develop the habit of answering three questions before beginning to write. Yes, you must answer them all. This system reminds me of a team of lawyers carefully building their case for a jury trial. You have to tell the jury what to think. But you also have to tell them why they should think that, and then you have to back it up with some good evidence.

The three questions:

1. **What do I *think*?** (What do you believe and want the reader to remember, learn, or come to believe?)

2. **Why do I think that?** (What led you to draw that conclusion or to come to that position and belief?)

3. **Can I show any evidence?** (This is where facts, information, and observation come in.)

Now you're ready to write and to lay out your case to convince every reader to agree with you.

TIP #12. WRITE A DIARY FOR YOURSELF. WRITE EVERYTHING ELSE FOR THE READER.

The readers' mental images are what count. Not yours. Many writers (even some experienced adults) think that their job is to get their thoughts and ideas down onto paper—to write what they want to say. WRONG!

That kind of thinking is fine if you're writing it for yourself—if you're writing a personal journal or diary. But if you expect any other person to read what you write, then you are writing for *them* and not for yourself.

Why the distinction? You already know exactly what you want to write. You already have detailed, vivid images of it in your mind. Therefore, *any* words you write will be fine for you because almost any wording will pop those perfect images back up into your conscious mind since they already exist in your memory.

But some other reader knows nothing about your topic. They hold no pictures of it in their minds. They will rely exclusively on your writing to build those images. You have to write for *them*.

I was in a 4th grade classroom working with students on writing details. One boy wrote, "The dog went in the house." I asked him to add more details about the house and about the dog so that we could all see them in our minds. He looked at me as if I were the stupidest adult on Earth and said, "I don't need to write any more. I can already see them. It's my house and my dog!"

Your job is to add in the details that will make the reader (who doesn't know anything about you or your story) see images as clear and vivid as the ones you already hold.

It's not enough for *you* to be able to see them, yourself, when you read what you wrote—although that is a crucially important first step. You have to write so that every reader sees it as well as you do!

TIP #13. THERE IS NO "RIGHT" OR "WRONG" IN WRITING.

Students are eager to get the "right" answer and to be sure they didn't put down the "wrong" answer. However, when creating stories—or when writing in general—there is no "right" or "wrong." There is only "does it work?" or "doesn't it work?"

What do I mean? All that really matters in a written piece is: does this writing engage readers? Does it hold their attention? Does it create the vivid mental images that the writer intended? Does it convey the content (the story, the information) accurately into the mind and memory of the reader? That is what I mean by "does it work?"

There is no "one way" or "one particular wording" that accomplishes that lofty goal. There are ways to organize and present a story or essay that writers over the centuries have discovered work very well. They serve as excellent models of good writing. Still, that does not mean that those models are "right" and others are "wrong."

Rather than searching for a "right" way to write something, students will be better served to explore alternate ways to say the same thing and see which they like and which creates the most pleasing response from their readers.

CHAPTER 3

WRITING WORKOUTS

Workout #1: The BIG Three

Quick Summary & Purpose

** **Purpose:** • Demonstrate the power of beginning a story with core character information.

Summary: If students begin their stories by creating core character information, they greatly increase the probability that they will produce a successful story. However, this isn't a "natural" place for students to start. They want to start by creating plot, the surest way to undermine their own story. This workout helps them establish a new and better habit.

Key Grades

Excellent for all grades

Time Required

Part 1: 15 to 20 minutes. Regular repetition is recommended.
Part 2: 15 to 30 minutes

Introduction

Students typically want to start their story creation by creating a plot line—the action, what happens. It is the surest way to create boring stories. It is a formula for reader boredom. It is important to shift their most basic thinking away from plot and **_to characters_**. This workout represents a big step along that pathway.

Directions

Bring three students to the front of the class and announce that they are going to create a story for the class.

Each student will create one of the three core character elements: identify the main character, define that character's goal, and create obstacles and problems. However, the specific wording you use in soliciting these bits of information is important.

The goal of this exercise is to demonstrate that these three essential character elements always launch and define a story. Reinforce that concept regularly.

The wording I have found that works the best is as follows.

To the first student: "The other two students are going to make up a story. All you have to do is make up that first, most important, bit of information they need, which is . . ." Here I pause to let student and class mull over what information should come first. "Which is . . . the character.

From *Writing Workouts to Develop Common Core Writing Skills: Step-by-Step Exercises, Activities, and Tips for Student Success, Grades 7–12* by Kendall Haven. Santa Barbara, CA: Libraries Unlimited. Copyright © 2015.

Every story needs to start with *who* the story is going to be about. This character you're going to make up can be, but doesn't have to be, a human being. It does have to be a fictional, never before made up, character. It could be an animal—a dog, a frog, an elephant, a snake, a snail, or a mosquito. It could be a bush or a tree. It doesn't even have to be alive. It could be a cloud, a chair, or your shoelace. You can have them make up a story about anything. But it does have to be a brand-new fictional character. What do you want them to make up a story about?"

Let student #1 now create a character's first impression: the species identity, name, age, and just enough physical information so everyone envisions the same character. You can veto any character you don't like. I always veto aliens because it takes too much background information for everyone to understand the species, their world, and their basic life patterns and needs. Also veto all previously created fictional characters and any attempt to use real people (or model a fictional character after a real person—most often a classmate).

You repeat and summarize whatever they pick. "Once there was a young, floppy-eared rabbit named Seymore."

To the second student: "Now the second bit of essential character information: *In this story*, what did Seymore need to either do or get? It doesn't have to be anything that would make sense for a rabbit to want to do or get. He could *want* to do *anything*. What do you want Seymore to **need**—to be after—in this story?"

Your wording here is important. If you ask for the character's goal (what you really want), you'll get nothing but blank stares. Ask for what the character needs to either do or get and you'll get great answers.

Again summarize the created information thus far. "Once, there was an old, floppy-eared rabbit named Seymore who wanted to eat some chocolate chip ice cream. He was tired of carrots and lettuce. He was tired of always going to the salad bar. He wanted dessert. He wanted some ice cream!"

To the third student: "Now the third bit of essential character information. Why hasn't Seymore gotten any ice cream? What's keeping Seymore from getting his ice cream? Something must, or he'd already have it. So what's keeping Seymore from getting any ice cream?"

You are asking for obstacles, either problems or conflicts. The wording shown above will spark their creation. Asking directly for a problem or obstacle typically won't.

Allow the student to make up three or four potential obstacles. Stop the student anytime he or she drifts into a plotting sequence (a series of events that could happen in the story). You want only the potential obstacles, not how they will fit into the story.

Again summarize for the class. "Once there was an old, floppy-eared rabbit named Seymore who wanted to eat some chocolate chip ice cream. He was tired of carrots and lettuce. He wanted dessert. He wanted some ice cream! BUT, Seymore had no money to buy ice cream.

And his mother said he couldn't have any because it was bad for him and would rot his teeth. Besides, the ice cream store owner hated rabbits and would shoot any rabbit that came near his store. But Seymore *really* wanted some ice cream."

If you find (as most often happens) that this student has created only problems confronting the character (e.g., he has no money, he doesn't know where the ice cream store is, etc.), ask, "**Who** doesn't want Seymore to get his ice cream?" This will always shift their focus from problems to conflicts.

Now turn to the class and ask, "How is this story going to end? What's the last thing that will happen at the end of this story?"

They will answer, "It ends when Seymore gets some ice cream." Most likely, they will try to include the plotting sequence that explains *how* Seymore will get his ice cream. Cut such discussion short. You want only what happens at the very end.

Now say, "Getting ice cream is one of two possible endings for this story. Does anyone know the other?" The other, of course, is that Seymore *never* gets any ice cream. It usually takes a while for students to come up with this option. If any suggest that the story ends when Seymore dies (and 4th, 5th, and 6th grade boys surely will), ask if, after he dies, Seymore still wants some ice cream. That will fit their answer back into one of the two plausible endings for the story.

The main character's goal defines the story's end and creates structure for the story. Stories end when the main character's primary goal is resolved—one way or the other.

Open up the discussion for other possible obstacles and problems, both internal and external. Stop anyone who begins to present a plotting scenario. They should only be allowed to suggest other obstacles that could keep the character from reaching his or her goal.

As a class, discuss which obstacles will make for a better story. Consistently it will be those obstacles that create the greatest risk and danger for the character. Risk and danger create the excitement and tension every story needs to propel a reader through to a powerful and satisfying climax.

Ask if any students think they know how the story will go. Many will say yes. Don't allow them to launch into their version of the story. Rather, ask them *why* they think they know how the story goes. The discussion will lead back to the chosen obstacles.

Obstacles create plot.

Part 2: The Big 3 *Plus*

Back to student #2. Ask, "Why does Seymore want ice cream?" You are now searching for motives to support the goal. Let the whole class participate. Note for the class that any suggested motives that make the goal more critically imperative create *suspense* and greatly increase interest in the story.

Finally, if time permits, turn back to student #1 and say, "Seymore (our character) isn't very interesting to me yet. I don't know enough about him to care one way or the other. Tell me something interesting about Seymore."

This launches the class into an exploration of character traits. I usually take control of this discussion and write categories of character information on the board one at a time and let students create four or five traits for each. Those that I typically present (in this order) are: fears, flaws and frailties (I start with allergies and then go to physical imperfections), things the character is good at (including academic subjects); things he is bad at (can't do well), physical description, things he's done that he is proud of, things he's done that he is ashamed of, passions and loves, things he hates, etc. You may use whatever categories you want. See the "Character Trait" section in *Get It Write!* for a listing of potential categories.

You will find that the class goes wild for this activity. Ideas fly. Everyone thinks of more outrageous answers than the next person. Your jobs are:

1. Make sure that all suggestions are plausible and fit the category you are working on. I demand that students explain any answer that doesn't make good sense to me. (If, for example a student says that the character is allergic to air, I demand to know why he hasn't already taken care of this allergy since he has always been exposed to air. I also demand specifics on what the effect of the allergy would be.)

2. Play scribe and ringmaster. Keep order and keep the lists moving.

3. Point out to the class how much fun it is to create character traits. Most of them think of this task as boring drudgery. But no! This is where authors pump fun, energy, and delight into their stories.

During the whole exercise your job is to keep the story moving and to prevent students from interjecting plot. No plot is mentioned or discussed during this exercise. However, once these basic character elements have been created, every student intuitively "knows" what has to happen in the story.

Post-Activity Review and Discussion

Creating character always creates an effective story. Creating a plot (a series of actions) does not. One of the most valuable writing habits you can instill in your students is to always start with character, goal, motive, and interesting character traits; then expand to problems and conflicts; and only then to the action and plot.

Quick Summary & Purpose

** **Purpose:** • Develop a sense of character and character reaction.
           • Develop a feel for pre- and post-event descriptive power.
           • Develop a good feel for momentary character sensory perceptions.

Summary: Each student writes a short in-class essay that starts with them getting into BIG TROUBLE. This writing develops their ability to create character and to succinctly link cause-and-effect time sequencing in their writing.

Key Grades

Excellent for all grades.

Time Required

30 minutes on day 1 for the writing. 30 to 45 on day 2 for sharing and review.

Introduction

This is one of the most fun writing assignments students ever receive. They can all relate to it and are energized to pour some effort into their writing. The learning comes both from this exuberant writing effort and from the sharing and analysis of the sensory details that build a real, engaging, and credible scene.

Directions

Stand in front of the class with a large open surface (desk or table) in front of you. Say these words and, at the indicated moment, slam you hand (open, palm down) hard on that open surface. The more noise from this slam, the better.

"You walk home, happy, content. All is right with the world. You think nothing can go wrong. You step up onto your front porch. You smile and open the door . . .. And, WHAM!!!!! (slam here) instantly you perceive that you are in BIG trouble (B-I-G trouble).

Here is the resulting writing assignment:

Assignment: *Write the story that begins at that moment. How do you know you're in trouble? What do you think, sense, feel, say, do? Explain—going forward and backwards—from that moment of revelation, to make it a story.*

Now let them write.

They must start just where you started: with themselves happily approaching their own front door without a care in the world. After establishing that wonderful moment when they realize that they are in BIG TROUBLE, they can back fill as needed to develop the situation, and move forward toward resolution of the event.

I typically give intermediate grades 30 to 40 minutes to write. I have found that all students—even the most reluctant writers—respond enthusiastically to this writing prompt.

Post-Activity Review and Discussion

Read all student writing overnight, and select three or four to be read to the class. Let these students read their own writing out loud the next day.

Guide any follow-on discussion to two topics:

1. The sensory detail at the moment the front door is opened. Note how those pieces that really suck listeners in provide detailed information about what the student at the door saw, heard, felt, sensed, and otherwise perceived. (See TIP #8: TFSS.)

2. Detailed and believable pre- and post-moment descriptions. That is, effective writing sets listeners up for the key moments and then allows us to watch the aftermath of those moments.

I prefer not to grade this activity. However, if grades are to be assigned, they should be based on the depth and breadth of detail used to describe the moment of realization after opening the front door, and on the character development in the pre- and post-revelation development of the complete story.

There is no absolute need to have students rewrite their essays. However, following class discussion, this is a good opportunity to allow students to revise, edit, and *then* rewrite their essay.

Workout #3: How to Make a Better Peanut Butter & Jelly Sandwich

Quick Summary & Purpose

** **Purpose:** • Develop an awareness of the need for precision in writing description.
  • Develop a feel for the persuasive power of detailed imagery and the dual need for evocative sensory description combined with precise physical detail in order to build vivid, alluring, engaging, and powerful images in readers' minds.
  • Appreciate the process and power of adding details during revision & editing.

Summary: All they have to do is write down directions for making a better peanut butter & jelly sandwich. However, each student will quickly become aware of the extent to which they write for themselves (and what *they* know) and not for the reader (and what *they* know). They will also clearly see the power of sensory images and details to guide readers' interpretation of their writing.

Key Grades

Excellent for all grades

Time Required

15-20 minutes on each of three successive days

Introduction

This is a three-step writing workout. Do not reveal that future steps even exist until they are actually being assigned.

Directions

Step 1: The Basics

   This step starts with a deceivingly simple assignment

Assignment: *By the numbers, write detailed directions for making the best-ever PB&J sandwich.*

That's the assignment. If they ask for clarification, say that you want them to write down in exact sequential order each step for making what they think is the ideal (the best) peanut butter & jelly sandwich. Yes, they can (even should) number the steps as they write them.

That should be sufficient. Have them double space when they write these directions.

From *Writing Workouts to Develop Common Core Writing Skills: Step-by-Step Exercises, Activities, and Tips for Student Success, Grades 7–12* by Kendall Haven. Santa Barbara, CA: Libraries Unlimited. Copyright © 2015.

Students must save all of their writing for this activity. They will write their directions three times. The most powerful teaching will come at the end when they compare the three versions.

Set a time limit for their writing. I usually use 10-15 minutes for high school and middle school classes.

Invariably, someone will claim to hate PB&J sandwiches. For them, the best PB&J is the one you make and then throw away. But they still have to write directions for making that sandwich first. Instead of eating the sandwich as the final direction, these writers will instruct readers to throw it in the garbage and eat something else.

Evaluation & Post Discussion

Overnight, look *very literally* at what each student has written and try to identify the unstated assumptions each has made. Identify as many of these on each student's page as you can. Don't grade the papers at this point. Comment only on—but profusely on—the imprecision of their directions.

Many, for example, will say to get the peanut butter out of the refrigerator and spread it on the bread without instructing you to close the refrigerator, unscrew the lid of the peanut butter jar, get a spreading knife (or table knife) from the silverware drawer, and to use that knife to do the scooping and spreading. Many will omit telling you where to place the bread once you have retrieved it from its wrapper (on the counter? on the floor? in the sink? etc.).

Be as picky as you dare, based on the writing competency level of your students.

Next day, you will need to bring to school a loaf of bread, a jar of peanut butter and several knives (including at least one that would not work well at all for use in making a peanut butter & jelly sandwich).

Return the papers; give students a chance to look over all of your notes and marks; and then start a discussion with this live demonstration:

Find one of their papers that mentioned neither taking the bread out of the loaf wrapper nor unscrewing the jar of peanut butter. (A typical direction says, "Put the bread on a plate and put the peanut butter on it with a knife.")

Read such a direction and, as you do, place the entire loaf of bread on a plate (unopened) and place the jar of peanut butter (unopened) and a knife on top of it. You have accurately and literally followed their direction. Ask the class if you have now successfully made a PB&J sandwich.

As an alternative, students rarely provide specific details on how to assemble the sandwich once peanut butter has been spread on one piece of bread and jelly on the other. Most say, "Put the two pieces together." Fine. For your demo, slap the bread together with the jelly and peanut butter on the outside.

You get the idea of the demo. Do as many as you want. Literally and exactly follow a student's written directions to demonstrate the lack of precise and complete details. These demos are fun to watch and graphically point out the serious lackings in the level of detail students provided.

Now launch a discussion along these core themes:

1. The Curse of Knowledge. Each student already holds a detailed mental image of each step. *Any* words they write will pull that picture into their minds and *seem* to be totally adequate. Whatever they write will make perfect sense to them—because they already know! The "trick" to successful writing is figuring out what you have to write so that someone who doesn't already know will form the same mental images that you already hold.

2. What do the readers really need? Why can't they see it as well as you? Discuss what information (in general) readers need in order to form vivid, interesting mental images. Have students try to identify (from their own reading experience) what pops rich and engrossing pictures into their minds while they read.

Step 2: Give Me Details or Give Me Reading Death!

It's time to rewrite their directions.

Assignment: *Rewrite your directions, being clear and precise so that anyone will be able to follow them and successfully make a PB&J sandwich.*

Use the same time limit as before. No other directions or discussion should be needed.

Evaluation & Post-Discussion

Again overnight, read these version 2 directions to make sure that they have significantly increased the specificity of, and level of, detail in their directions. There is no need to comment back to each student on this version. In this version, they typically focus on physical, factual details. These often read as if the student were giving directions to a robot. However, in so doing, they typically overlook describing their sensory experience and reaction to the process and to their sandwich. The writing is usually much more accurate. But it is not engaging, not compelling and is, well, typically boring.

Lead a short in-class discussion on what makes a narrative exciting and fun to read. It is not the action (in this case, the culinary directions). It is the character and sensory detail that places vivid images in our minds and sets us up to be excited by the other elements in a story.

Step 3. The Sales Pitch

Time for the students to make one final rewrite of their directions. The goal of this rewrite is to move from precision to engaging and persuasive.

Assignment: *Rewrite your directions one more time. In this rewrite, convince me that yours is the best, the most delicious, mouth-watering PB&J recipe in the world. Convince me that I should pick your PB&J directions as my all-time favorite meal, as my mouth-watering ideal. Convince me that I will adopt your directions as the only way I will ever again want to prepare a PB&J sandwich.*

They write their directions a third time, focusing this time not on the factual directions—supposedly already there—but on the reader's sensory experience of both the process and the product.

Here are three cueing questions that I often read (or hand out) to help them think of strong, visceral description.

1. What does the sandwich remind you of?

2. What does it feel like, smell like, and taste like in your hands and in your mouth? What does it sound like when you take a bite? Is it messy or neat to eat? Does the jelly ooze out the side and trickle down your fingers and arm?

3. Hunt for GREAT action verbs to describe each step and action in the process (ones like smear, smoosh, glob, smother, slap, splat, or slather instead of dull ones like "put" or "spread").

Post-Activity Review and Discussion

Both you and each student should compare the three versions. Which is the most fun to read? Which engages you and holds your attention? Look at powerful, forceful words and images in version #3 compared to the bland and uninteresting words in version #1. Now revisit the discussion on what builds a vivid image. What makes you want to read something? What holds your attention?

While you can grade either the quality of each student's version #3 writing or (I think preferably) the improvement from version #1 to version #3, I think this is best kept as an ungraded—but powerful—demonstration of students' natural writing style (version #1) and the impact of focused revision and editing (version #3).

Quick Summary & Purpose

** **Purpose:** • Learn what does—and what does not—create story excitement.

Summary: This is a fun writing assignment that forces students to make something ordinary and mundane still seem to be exciting to the reader. Once this concept and writing technique are learned, they work on and for all types of writing and for any and all writing assignments.

Key Grades

Excellent for all grades

Time Required

Introduction & Writing: 30 minutes
Review, Sharing & Discussion: 15 to 30 minutes

Introduction

All students long to make their stories (and other narratives) exciting. They crave the glory of producing something others call "exciting." Most, sadly, fail time and time again.

Why such pervasive and widespread failure? Simply put, it is because students ignore the writing elements that really do create excitement and try to force writing elements to create excitement that are not capable of accomplishing that grand feat.

First, what is excitement? It is a feeling, an emotion manifested in the mind of a reader. Excitement is actually a momentary expression of anticipatory tension. Excitement exists in close anticipation of an action and dissipates quickly after that action is completed.

Second, what *doesn't* create excitement? Action. The actions and events in a story cannot, will not, and never have—in and of themselves—created excitement. Most students believe that action does create excitement because they feel that excitement during action sequences. However, the excitement isn't created by the action. No. It is created by other writing elements that then come to fruition and are experienced during subsequent action events.

Third, what *does* create excitement? That question is the exact point of this workout. Of the Eight Essential Elements of effective narratives (see TIP #5), it is Risk and Danger that create the feeling we call excitement. If nothing can go wrong, if story characters anticipate no conflicts or risks, then readers will feel no excitement.

Directions

Tell the class that they are going to write a personal essay based on this prompt:

Assignment*: You're walking home from school, and on that walk absolutely nothing exciting happens. It's just a walk to home during which nothing unusual, or in any way out of the ordinary, happens. Write an essay describing this walk to home . . . and make your essay exciting to read.*

The Rules

1. Students must use actual streets, buildings, and places they would normally see on their walk home.

2. They will write this as a first draft (double space), but should not worry about editing or spell checking during this writing period

3. They MUST make their essay exciting. Most students (if not all) will instantly object and argue that if nothing exciting *happens*, they won't be able to write an exciting essay. You should respond by saying, *"The rules stand, nothing exciting can actually happen during the walk but, yes, you can make the essay you write exciting."* Let them struggle with that seeming contradiction. However, it isn't a contradiction at all, and during the post-writing discussion you will be able to use their writing to clearly demonstrate what makes writing exciting.

Post-Activity Review and Discussion

Collect the essays and evaluate them overnight. Many (often most) will try to sneak "exciting" action into their essay. Cross it out in bold red marker. Look for those who have kept to the rules.

In class, lead a discussion about what creates narrative excitement. If the readers perceive that real risk and danger exist for a character, whatever that character does will be exciting.

Example: *Walking up the front steps to the porch of your house is not exciting. But what if the reader knows that a pressure-sensitive bomb has been placed under the third step? The person walks up the curving walkway and steps up onto the first step. He steps up onto the second step . . . He . . . a car horn honk makes him turn around and step back one step as he waves at a passing neighbor. He steps back up on the second step. He lifts his foot to step again . . . but pauses as his barking dog romps around the corner of the house, tail wagging. He turns back toward the house and lifts his foot to step up onto the third step. . . . But then remembers that he has to close the garage and steps down again. . . . See how eminent risk and danger create the excitement?*

However, if nothing out of the ordinary happens, if there are no secretly planted bombs, how can a writer create excitement? By creating risk and danger **in the mind of their character**.

The best source of excitement is to let readers see into the mind (thinking) of a character. Their worries, fears, anxieties create the excitement readers need.

Example: *I walk along the sidewalk of 3rd Street next to that row of storefronts between Jones and Montague. A dog on the other side of the street is . . . is watching me . . . A big dog. . . . I think a Doberman. . . . I think he's glaring at me. . . . And he's not on a leash! At any moment he'll pull back his lips and growl. I'll see yellow, blood-stained killer teeth. He could dash over here in three seconds! He'll rip me apart! And I'm trapped against these lousy storefronts. All the doors are locked. Why do the stores all have to close up at 5:00 PM? I'm trapped out here to die all alone torn into a thousand shreds by a vicious yellow-eyed killer. . . . Wait. He's not opening his mouth to bare his fangs. Just to lick his master's hand. . . . And look! He is on a leash. I hadn't noticed it before. It's black like the dog. . . . They're walking off down the street. . . . I . . . I get to live!*

This brings up the second teaching point of this exercise (See TIP #8). To allow readers inside the mind of a character, writers must think in TFSS terms. (TFSS stands both for the mnemonic "Thursday, Friday, Saturday, Sunday" and for the key internal character information "Think, Feel, Sense, Say."—what a character thinks, how he feels, how he senses (perceives) the scenes around him, and what he says. It is through these bits of moment-by-moment internal character information that readers become aware of that internal character world that creates true story excitement.

Use as many student examples from student essays as you can of sentences and even phrases that delve into this internal character world. Allow other students to react and to reflect on the two key concepts of this exercise: risk and danger, and the internal character musings revealed through TFSS—both the keys to narrative excitement.-

As a final option, have students rewrite their essays based on what they learned from the class discussion. Read and compare the two essay versions.

Workout #5: Make the Moment Real

Quick Summary & Purpose

** **Purpose**: • Teach the skill of making moments and events experientially *real* for readers.

Summary: Many students fail to include adequate sensory detail because the sweep and scope of their stories is too vast or grand to allow for focused detail within the available writing time limits. This workout forces them to consider only a single momentary event and to concentrate all of their writing onto those several seconds of time and onto a tightly defined single spot. The result is a powerful demonstration of effective experiential writing.

Key Grades

Excellent for all grades

Time Required

Step 1 Writing: Oral prep (optional) 15 minutes
                 45 minutes to write
                 30 to share, review, and revise
Step 2 Writing: same time requirement

Introduction

This is an exercise in crafting moment-by-moment sensory detail. More specifically, students must write exquisite sensory detail through the eyes of a character. This is where the TFSS tip (TIP #8) comes in handy. The details students write reflect the minute perceptions, reactions, and feelings of a character, as perceived and felt through the sensory organs of that character.

Directions

Step 1

Begin with this straightforward writing assignment:

Assignment: *Describe—in great detail—one specific event: jumping off of a 30-foot-high rock into a lake.*

There is nothing magic about that exact assignment. Use alternatives if you like. However, those alternatives should avoid anything that would be life threatening or typically result in serious injury. Still it should be something that gets the heart pumping.

If you use the 30-foot leap into water, see if you can find a spot where students can experience standing 30 feet up. A five-meter diving board in the school pool is halfway up to 30 feet.

Here are the rules for this writing workout.

1. Students will write in first person.

2. Their writing goal is to make us feel every aspect and moment—every heart-pounding fear and thrill—of the jump and those fleeting few moments in the air. They must make us vividly live each moment with them throughout this jump.

Refer back to TIP #8: Think, feel, sense, and say as a guide for this writing. Encourage students to use all senses as they describe this event.

No, it doesn't matter if some students have never done it. They can imagine it. No one will fact check their work. It's the sensory detail writing we are after.

I usually assign a minimum work limit for this activity (instead of a maximum time limit)—at least 200 words. More commonly, 300 in high school classes. I always want students to know that the only way they will meet that word quota is to delve into minute sensory detail—something they rarely (if ever) get to do. Thus, this is an aspect of effective writing most never have had the chance to experience

The optional oral prep is to do a One-on-One-on-One-on-One about this jump (see Workout #20).

I usually allow a full period for the initial writing. If students claim to be finished, ask if they have met the minimum work count. (They rarely will have.) Encourage them to delve deeper into the moment-to-moment character feeling, sensations, and reactions.

Allow several students to read their essays. Briefly discuss. What was effective? What grabbed your attention? What made you feel it and see it? (Be specific.) What held you (and what didn't)?

Allow students to review and revise their own writing. Their goal: crank up the emotion in their description!

Step 2

Repeat the assignment. However, this time you will use something they have **never done** (parachute from 20,000 feet; wrestle with an alligator; deliver a speech —or sing—to a stadium filled with 50,000 people, etc.). Their writing goal is exactly the same as in step 1: make us feel every aspect and moment. Make us vividly live each moment with you. Here they will have to rely not on their experience and memory, but on their imagination and writing skill to make the event feel as experiential as was their writing in step 1.

Skip the oral prep for this step and have students dive straight into the writing. Again allow a full period for this writing so that they will have time to delve into their imagined moment-to-moment sensations, experience, feelings, and reactions.

Post-Activity Review and Discussion

Allow several students to read their essays. Search for great description—writing that paints a rich and vivid picture and that also reveals character. Discuss the nature of effective details—both character details and sensory details.

What drew them into listening about these descriptions? What made you feel it? Be specific. Pick three or four mediocre bits of description and, as a class, orally improve them. As a class, build up a list of the characteristics of effective detail.

Workout #6: My Favorite Season

Quick Summary & Purpose

** **Purpose:** • Learn the advantages of oral development of details and personal positions.
• Learn the persuasive power of relevant sensory details

Summary: This workout is couched as a class debate/discussion about which is the "best" season. Students are required to take a stance and justify their choice both verbally (in small groups) and in writing. The format allows them to watch how the quality and persuasiveness of their writing grows over the course of each step.

Key Grades

Excellent for 7th to 10th. Good for 11 & 12.

Time Required

Step 1: 5 minutes
Step 2: 15 to 20 minutes
Step 3: 30 minutes
Discussion: 15 to 30 minutes

Introduction

Through a long series of student interviews, I have found that students see events they write about much more clearly, and in much more detail, in their minds than they ever put on the page when they write. I have found that the problem is that they begin to write before they have fully and concretely developed their mental images. Thus, the writing reflects this mental fuzziness.

This is an activity designed to show students how much easier it is to write compelling imagery and argument if they first take the time to orally develop and refine those images in their own minds.

Directions

This is a three-step exercise.

Step 1. The Initial Writing

Have every student, at their seat, decide which of the four basic seasons is their favorite (spring, summer, fall, or winter) and write down three or four reasons for why it is their favorite. They must save these pieces of paper.

Step 2. The Oral Arguments

Designate one of the four corners of the room for each season, and instruct everyone to go to the corner that corresponds to their favorite.

The group of students clustered in each corner must first identify one student as discussion leader and one student as group spokesperson. The leader will be charged to lead a group discussion during which that group of students will lay out all of the reasons why their chosen season is the best and should be picked as *everybody's* favorite.

The spokesperson must take notes and be prepared to orally argue why their season is the best.

I usually give groups five minutes to accomplish this organization and compilation of their arguments. I often circulate to those groups with the fewest students to make sure they have strong arguments for why their season is the best.

Now, one at a time, the spokesperson for each season steps forward and presents his or her arguments. You act as debate moderator. After each season's spokesperson has presented his or her case, allow the spokesperson for each of the other three seasons to offer one—only one—argument for why they *don't* like the season of the spokesperson who just presented.

Allow no other discussion or side comment during these oral arguments.

Step 3.

Students return to their seats. They will now write a persuasive essay arguing that everyone should agree with their pick of the best season.

Before they are allowed to write, they should look at (and revise if they want to) their list of reasons why their pick is the best season.

Having revised that list, they should turn two of their reasons into activities (***things to do*** that are representative of their reasons why this is the best season). Have students sketch a quick picture of each of these two activities. Technically, these are visual notes.

Finally, having heard from advocates of the other seasons, each student should write down one reason why he or she *doesn't* like each of the other three seasons.

Now—and only now—they are ready to write a persuasive essay arguing for why their season is the best. In that essay they will describe in vivid, compelling detail those two chosen activities and will include their reasons for disliking the other three seasons.

Post-Activity Review and Discussion

Students can now compare that first piece of paper listing their three or four reasons for choosing one season to their final essay.

Discuss with the class what benefit they gained from the time spent on oral argument and on sketching those two pictures. Create first; write second.

Workout #7: The What-Makes-It-Real Game

Quick Summary & Purpose

** **Purpose:** • Demonstrate that specific, relevant story details create a sense of reality more than anything else a student can put in their story.

Summary: By turning a review of what makes a story sound real into a mystery game, students are compelled to sift through a story for all possible clues without even realizing that they are creating a short list of elements to include in their own stories to make them sound equally real.

Key Grades

Excellent for all grades.

Time Required

15–18 minutes for the game; 15–20 for the follow-on discussion

Introduction

It is a key question: how do authors make their writing *seem* real to readers—whether or not it actually is about real places and events? Every fiction story needs to seem as real to the mind of the reader as if it had actually happened. How do student authors create that kind of "reality" in their writing? That is the focus of this workout.

Directions

Divide the class into groups of either three or four. Give each student a moment to recall a personal (real) story on whatever topic you assign. Use simple, broad topics—something funny that happened to you, something that happened when you were six or seven, or something scary. Even a topic as broad as something that happened in your family will work well.

Three rules:

1. These personal and family stories **MUST** have actually happened.

2. They **MUST** have happened at least three years ago.

3. These stories **MUST** *not* have been previously shared with other students in the class.

Each student shares with their group the bare-bones summary of their remembered story. Some students will want to drift into elaborate storytelling here. Don't let them. These should be 20- to 30-second summaries. Give the group a total of two minutes and task them to keep on time. Remind each group not to allow anyone from another group hear anything they say about these stories.

Only after this time has elapsed, instruct each group to choose one of these stories that they think makes the best story, or the one that is their favorite. They cannot combine stories to create a new super-story. They must pick one of the actual stories told by a group member. Give them 30 seconds to accomplish this.

Proceed only after every group has picked their story. Tell the class that every member of the group must now learn that one story they picked well enough so that they could tell it as if it had happened to them. This means that each group member has to question the person to whom it really happened to uncover the information they will need to tell the story.

At your option, you can prompt them about what kind of information they need to master. When and where did it happen? Who was there? What happened? Why? How did the characters feel? Why? etc.

Be sure to tell them that they may adjust the physical reality of the story to be plausibly consistent with their own history. For example, if the story happened between the teller and a brother, a child who doesn't have a brother could say the story happened with a cousin. Who would know the child doesn't have a male cousin?

If the story happened when the teller lived in Atlanta, and the other students never lived in Atlanta, they can say it happened where they really lived at the appropriate time. If Atlanta were important to the story, they would then say it happened while their family was visiting someone (grandmother, friend, etc.) in Atlanta. Again, who would know it wasn't true?

Give the groups 75 to 90 seconds to gather whatever information they need.

You now pick one group. All the members of that group line up at the front of the class and, one by one, tell the complete story, each claiming as they do that it really did happen to them. Instruct each teller that the goal is to say and do whatever is necessary to convince every person in the room that the story really *did* happen to the teller. That's the teller's job.

The job of the audience is to figure out to whom it really happened. Don't allow any pause for discussion between tellers. As soon as teller #1 finishes, say, "And now the story from teller #2."

As soon as all the tellers have finished and the thunderous applause has died away, have the audience vote by show of hands for the teller they think the story really happened to. Do not allow any discussion before this vote. Every student must commit themselves and vote.

Usually the biggest vote-getter is not the person to whom the story really happened.

Post-Activity Review and Discussion

This is a fun game and does develop oral storytelling skills. But the real value of this exercise comes from the following discussion. Ask the class, "Why did you vote the way you voted? It doesn't matter if you voted for the right person or not. I still want to know why you thought one story sounded more real than the others."

Write the responses you get on the board spatially dividing them into two groups: those comments that relate to the story and those that relate to the way the story was told.

Discuss those elements that made the story seem real enough to vote for. Those are extremely powerful story elements for each student to remember to include in their stories.

As you repeatedly use this exercise, vary the story theme. Any commonly available experience will do—summer vacation, time they were scared, something that happened on a bike, disasters with a pet (theirs or someone else's), etc.

Amazingly, I find that every audience votes for the same few reasons. It doesn't much matter if they are teachers, 5th graders, or college seniors. Even more amazing, almost all groups mention their reasons for voting in the same order.

First is always *details* in the story. One teller included more details and his story sounded more real. One teller included impossible or unlikely details and so sounded less real. Details create reality.

The second aspect mentioned usually has to do with the *way* the story was told. One teller over-acted, or hesitated and seemed to be making it up. One teller put more expression in the story, or seemed more confident and so was more believable. One seemed more natural and relaxed. One seemed stiffer and more halting. The general impression created by the way the teller told the story seemed more real or less real and so he or she was either voted for or against.

Next mentioned is usually something about characters and the amount of character information one person included. Next is usually humor. Make a list of all the reasons your students mention. It will be a very short list. There are not many things an audience needs in order to enjoy a story.

What makes a story enjoyable are the same few elements that make it sound real. Alone at the top of these lists are story details and that the teller seemed comfortable with, and enthused about, their own story.

Workout #8: I Love It; I Hate It!

Quick Summary & Purpose

** **Purpose**: • Learn the role of a character's thoughts and reactions in creating voice and in revealing character personality.

Summary: This is another workout in refining student mastery of voice. This time, however, student writers will focus not on the actual words a character says, but on how the character reacts to, and thinks about, events and situations.

Key Grades

Excellent for all grades

Time Required

Writing: 30 minutes
Review & Discussion: 15 to 20 minutes

Introduction

What does it mean to have a *voice*? What makes one voice different from another? Discuss this as a class before you proceed.

"Voice" refers to a combination of two things: **what** someone says and **how** they say it. The vocabulary characters uses (big words, mono-syllabic utterances, lots of adjectives, no modifiers, the word "like" or "basically" in every sentence, etc.) and how they phrase and construct what they say (short, choppy sentences; long run-together sentences, etc.). These are aspects of what a character says.

Volume, tone, pitch, breathiness, speed, etc.—these are all aspects of how characters say what they say.

Combine those two and you have a voice.

Question: how do student writers create unique, specific, interesting voices for their characters? Decide what a character would say and wouldn't say—as well as what the character would and wouldn't think. Then decide on the character's emotional state—how he feels. Let that emotion dictate how the character says what he says.

This fun writing workout will clearly demonstrate both the techniques and the allure of effective character voices.

From *Writing Workouts to Develop Common Core Writing Skills: Step-by-Step Exercises, Activities, and Tips for Student Success, Grades 7–12* by Kendall Haven. Santa Barbara, CA: Libraries Unlimited. Copyright © 2015.

Directions

Students will write two half-page descriptive stories, one at a time, each on its own piece of paper. These will be first-person stories. The student writer him- or herself will be the main character.

The first story will describe a typical, ordinary, everyday walk home from school (or other agreed-upon starting point). All of the places, sights, sounds, and occurrences in each story must be real, actual places and typical events and happenings.

While writing this first story, students will pretend that this walk is their favoritest thing to do in all the world. Pick specific (S-P-E-C-I-F-I-C) details along the walk, and show how the writer reacts to, and thinks/feels about, them.

The writer's job is to make it clear to readers of this paragraph that the writer *loves* this walk. Show us *exactly* what the student does on this walk, and make us know that this is the greatest, and most fun, thing he or she can imagine doing.

Give students 15 minutes to write.

Stop the writing and tell students that they will now rewrite their description of their walk home. In this second version, they MUST do exactly the same things, in the same order, and have exactly the same experiences as in the first paragraph. However, this time, they must write it so that it is clear to readers that the student loathes, hates, and despises this walk more than anything else the student can imagine.

Same walk. Same sights, sounds, and actions. But opposite feeling and reactions.

How will they communicate the difference? Through the voice (in this case the thoughts and reactions) of the writer.

Post-Activity Review and Discussion

Collect all papers and review their writing. Look for students who have created two clear personalities and viewpoints in their two paragraphs. Have several of these students read both paragraphs to the class.

As a class, discuss what specific language creates a sense of both the scene and the character. What language stayed the same? What changed? What was the effect of the changes? How does each paragraph build an expectation in your mind of what the character would do and say in other situations and settings?

Quick Summary & Purpose

** **Purpose:** • Learn how to make story characters interesting to readers.
  • Experience the failure of vague and general character description to engage and interest readers.

Summary: Students tend to write vague, general character descriptions. This is a workout to make that writing problem clear and conscious. Students will attempt to write interesting descriptions of three characters and, through the reactions they receive from fellow students, will learn exactly what is—and is not—interesting to readers.

Key Grades

Excellent for all grades

Time Required

15 minutes for the writing
20 to 30 minutes for the activity and discussion

Introduction

Readers are supposed to synthesize the specific bits of character detail provided by the writer into general conclusions ("He is funny," She is a liar," "He is good at sports," etc.). That's a reader's job. When students flip roles to become writers, they tend to carry that same old job with them. They write in general character conclusions ("He is weird," "She is nice," etc.).

This workout is designed to make them aware that, as writers, their job is to provide the specifics and let their readers do the synthesis work.

Directions

Each student needs a piece of paper. Along the left-hand margin they write "Family"; then indent below it and, on three successive lines, write 1, 2, and 3. Below that they write "Other" along the margin and again indent below it and write 1, 2, and 3. Drop down and write "Me" along the margin and 1, 2, and 3 below that.

Their paper now looks like this:

Family

1

2

3

Other

1

2

3

Me

1

2

3

You now instruct each student to select one family member.

Rules: It must be a person (no pets), but not the student him- or herself. It can be any relative (living or dead) as long as the student writer has actually met this person.

The student will now write three things (factual bits of information) about this selected family member that the student thinks are interesting on lines 1, 2, and 3 under "Family." Each item must be written in one sentence. Every statement must be true and accurate. Anything can qualify for inclusion as long as the student thinks it is something interesting about this specific person.

If students seem truly stuck, discuss possible categories of information as a class: physical traits, their history, possessions, hobbies or jobs, abilities and talents, disabilities, fears, hopes and dreams, friends and acquaintances, accomplishments . . . literally *anything* might make this person interesting.

Give students only a couple of minutes to write these three sentences.

Writing Rule: Students may *NOT* name the person in any of these three sentences. Use only third-person pronouns: "he" and "she."

Move to the next category, "Other." Students do the same thing, following the same rules for a person they know who is **not** related to them in any way.

Remind them that they may not name the person. Use only third-person pronouns "he" and "she."

Finally, now that they are getting used to writing interesting traits, they will write three things about themselves that they think would be interesting to a stranger meeting them for the first time.

Writing Rule: Students may **NOT** use "I" for any of these three sentences even though they are all about the student who is writing them. If the student is a girl, she writes "she." If a boy, write, "he." Use only third-person pronouns: "he" and "she."

I recommend that you do not model effective character description statements at this time. Students will simply all mimic what you said or wrote. However, for your use in guiding them to creating something to write down, here are a few common examples of ineffective and more effective description.

Note that the effective wording is always specific, vivid, and emphasizes what is different and unique about the character using images and terms that are (hopefully) a bit unusual.

Ineffective	Effective
He is funny.	He once made my grandmother laugh so hard she peed her pants.
She travels a lot.	She has been to all 50 states and to 11 foreign countries
He is good at sports.	He set a school record for both the 110-meter hurdles and the high jump.
She plays funny instruments.	She is so good at playing the harmonica with her nose that she was invited to play for the school board.
He does weird stuff.	He can write forward and backwards, and he plays spoons with his feet.

In-Class Analysis

Each student has now written nine character trait statements that they think are interesting (three each about three different people). Have students pick the three of those nine individual statements that they think are their three most interesting individual statements. It doesn't matter who these statements are about. These are simply what the student thinks are the three most interesting statements they wrote. (Could be two about one person and one about another. Could be one about each person. Doesn't matter.)

Students should star these three picks in the left-hand margin.

Now you need volunteers who will stand up and read those three starred statements. The class must focus not on the person, but on one, simple question: is this character trait statement interesting to me or not?

Here are the rules:

1. While reading, the student may not—even if asked—identify the person being described.

2. You want all three statements to sound the same so that students focus on the description. To do that, the reader will shift the gender of all three statements to his or her own gender no matter who the statements are about. If a boy gets up to read his three sentences, he will always use "he"—even if the statement is about his mother, sister, or aunt. If a girl gets up, she will always use "she"—again, even if the statement is about a male relative.

3. The first volunteer reads all three statements with no comment or discussion. Then have that student repeat the first statement. Have the class vote: It is interesting to me (thumbs up); it isn't interesting (thumbs down); or it's in-between (wiggling horizontal thumb).

4. Ask the class why they voted as they did. Make them be specific in justifying their vote. During this discussion the volunteer student may not add additional detail. Not yet.

5. Ask those who voted thumbs down or wiggly-horizontal thumb what they would do to make this statement more interesting. (Yes, you will now probably traipse into the realm of fiction. But that is alright for this activity.) Work with the class to make this one statement more interesting. Compare the idea behind each of their suggestions for how to improve the original statement with the qualities of effective character detail listed in the Post-Activity Discussion section.

6. Shift to the volunteer's second statement and repeat. If one of this student's statements seems tailor-made for rapid improvement (or, conversely, seems truly interesting), single that one statement out for class analysis.

7. Shift to another volunteer reader.

As you work through half-a-dozen statements that the class works to improve, watch for trends and patterns in how they make the sentences more interesting. Those will form a key part of the post-activity discussion and teaching.

Post-Activity Review & Discussion

Over the course of this workout you and your students will have used the important characteristics of interesting (effective) description as they work to create interesting character descriptions.

Good description is:

- **Specific** (as opposed to "general" and—more importantly—as opposed to "conclusion statements" about the character)

- **Unusual** (atypical characteristics, comparisons, or descriptors are always more interesting)
- **Unique** (a primary purpose of character traits is to differentiate this character from all others. Effective details show how this character is ***different***.)
- **Vivid** (character description that includes the sensory information that lets a reader form vivid mental imagery is always more interesting. The key word for creating vivid mental images is ***sensory information***.)

Quick Summary & Purpose

** **Purpose**: • Introduce the concept of sequels (character reflections)

Summary: Students tend to bounce from action to action, from scene to scene, without giving their characters (and readers) a chance to reflect on each piece of action. Sequels are quiet moments (no action) during which characters decide how they feel about the most recent event, what they think it means, and how it affects or redirects their planning and thinking for the future.

Key Grades

Good for all grades

Time Required

Oral Activity: 20 minutes
Written activity: 30 minutes

Introduction

Student stories tend to jump from action to action, from event to event. Overlooked are the critical character reactions to and reflections on these various events. While this information can be woven into the fabric of the story in a variety of ways, one consistently effective system (which has the side benefit of hammering home the necessity of tracking character reactions and reflections) is the scene and sequel system. This workout is a fun demonstration of that system.

Two definitions are in order.

Scene: a complete action, an event. Technically, a scene is like a mini-story. A character has some purpose (goal or intent), takes some action to achieve that purpose, has to struggle against some problem or obstacle, and finally, that action comes to some resolution at the end of the scene.

Sequel: a character's reflections on and feelings about the just concluded event, on how they interpret the meaning of the event, and on how it affects their view of and planning for the future. No action happens during a sequel. They are an opportunity for readers to peek into the thinking, internal processing, and planning of a central character.

Many (most) student writers fail to provide sequels after their events. Rather they tend to dive straight into the next event—thus depriving readers of all-important character insights. This workout dramatically shows the value and importance of sequels.

Directions

This exercise shows your students the power and reader allure of sequels by creating a game of the process of inserting sequels into a story line. First, discuss the concept of scenes and sequels and provide some examples from existing stories. Examples are included in the text.

This exercise is a demonstration game to do as a class. Assign one student to be Mr. Sequel. Initially, you may want to assume this role. Have a volunteer make up a character and initial core character information (goal, motive, key character traits, problems, etc.).

Once there was a young brown bear named Squirt who wanted some honey. But he was very small. So the other bears shoved him aside when they found a honeycomb and wouldn't let him have any. Even worse, Squirt couldn't climb trees, and so couldn't get his own honey from a beehive. But Squirt really wanted some honey.

That paragraph contains a character's first impression, a goal, and two obstacles. A second volunteer creates a scene. That is, an event or interaction involving this main character and the specified goal and obstacles.

One day Squirt saw a fat bee buzzing through the meadow and decided to follow it back to its hive. Maybe he'd find a way to get their honey.

But the bee angrily turned on Squirt. "Don't you follow me! I know you just want to steal our honey. But you can't have any. And if you try to get some, a thousand bees will sting and bite you and make you so miserable you'll wish you'd never heard of honey!" And the bee flew off.

That is a scene. We have character, intent (goal), conflict or problem, and action (character interaction) to address that problem, and a resolution to that action. Scenes are like mini-stories.

Now have Mr. Sequel step out of the room before several other volunteers guess at what might happen next. (If you are playing the role of Mr. Sequel, you should stay in the room.)

Guess #1: The bear swats and kills the bee.

Guess #2: The bear says he's not afraid of a bee and follows the bee home and pushes over the tree to get at the hive and the honey.

Guess #3: The bear is terrified and runs away to eat grubs.

Now bring Mr. Sequel back into the room and ask him to tell the class "how Squirt felt and what he thought after that first scene." (That is, ask Mr. Sequel to provide a sequel for that first scene.)

Squirt realized how mean and unfair it was for bears to steal honey from hardworking bees. He wanted honey, but realized he couldn't steal it from the bees. If he was going to get some honey he'd have to steal it from the humans at the grocery store.

That's a sequel. Nothing physically has happened in this sequel. Nothing should, except for the character reflecting on the previous scene, internalizing it, deciding what the action and interaction of the scene mean to them.

If Mr. Sequel includes any major actions taken by the main character, or any interactions with other characters, stop the sequel and correct this incursion of scene into sequel. Review with the class the difference between scene and sequel and the purpose of each.

Now the class can see how close or far-off the guesses were about what's most likely to actually happen in this story. That's the point of the exercise. The reason you send Mr. Sequel out of the room is so that the nature of the sequel he invents won't be influenced by other students' guesses about the action of the next scene.

Sequels lead us from scene to scene by showing how the main character interprets the last scene and plans for the next.

Have a volunteer now create the "real" next scene based on Scene #1 and its sequel.

Squirt went to the grocery store and asked for a job, claiming that he wanted to earn the money to buy his honey. He volunteered to be a stock boy, a cashier, even a sweeper. Really, he wanted to case the joint for a nighttime honey heist.

But the store owner said he didn't trust bears, and besides, health codes said bears weren't allowed in grocery stores because of all the moldy bear hair.

The owner said, "Go away!" and slammed the door in Squirt's face.

Note that a scene should have a purpose, some conflict or problem that is addressed, a character interaction, and a conclusion to that action or interaction.

Again have Mr. Sequel leave the room while several other students guess at what event might happen next. Mr. Sequel returns and reveals the next sequel, how Squirt feels about this last interaction, and what Mr. Sequel thinks it means to and for him.

Continue in this way through four or five scenes to the end of the story and a final sequel. Afterward hold a final class discussion on the role of, and importance of, sequels, and how the information presented in sequels helps us understand and sympathize with the main character. During the exercise, your job is to ensure that each student providing a scene presents a complete and valid scene but only one scene, that all offered scenes are consistent with story core information and past scenes and sequels, and that Mr. Sequel really does provide a plausible sequel following each scene. Some teachers task students to watch for, and point out, any improprieties in either the scenes or sequels supplied by other students.

Options/Variations

Many teachers act as Mr. Sequel for the first use of this exercise. It is key that the class sees real sequels. Before turning this important task over to students, you may want to model effective sequels yourself. Some teachers rotate the role of Mr. Sequel after each scene, allowing one student to provide only one sequel, and allowing more students the opportunity to try to create a sequel for the class.

Written Activity

Having seen the power of sequels in action during this oral exercise, you want to have students assess a sample of their own writing for the presence of sequels. Return copies of any piece of fiction writing that your students have turned in over the previous month or so. Use fiction writing for this exercise since student fiction writing is far more likely to be naturally organized into a series of scenes.

Have students physically draw dividing lines between scenes on this copy. Having done that, they should look for sequels either between scenes or along the margins of scenes.

Have students add sequels where they are missing and strengthen the emotional energy of the sequels they do already have.

Evaluate these sets of sequels and decide if further specific work on sequels is needed or if scene-and-sequel can become just another of the writing tools that you evaluate on the work they turn in.

Post-Activity Review and Discussion

The information in sequels in essential to our understanding of both character and story. We want to view all scenes through the eyes of the main character, but can only do that when we understand their interpretation of, and reaction to, the events of the story. That's a sequel.

Sequels are the intersection of the events of the previous scenes and the personality of the main character. Sequels reveal how character reflects on, and understands, events and action. Sequels lead the reader to understand and sympathize with character. If action is the "what" of a story, then sequels are the "so what."

Workout #11: Making It Relevant

Quick Summary & Purpose

** Purpose: • Use the events and emotions of a vivid personal experience to reinforce effective narrative planning and development steps and processes.

• Use the function of a central theme statement in design and planning of a narrative writing piece

Summary: Students tend to view the world through their own eyes (values, attitude, knowledge, etc.) when they write. Effective authors, however, try to look through the eyes of their characters **and of their intended audience**. Most students have never considered who will read their writing and how to engage and hold the attention of those readers. This workout will help.

Key Grades

Excellent for all grades

Time Required

Step 1: 15 minutes
Step 2: 20 minutes
Step 3: 20 to 30 minutes

Introduction

Especially when describing something traumatic that happened to themselves, most student writers think about . . . *themselves*. However, effective writers always—*always*—think about the reader. The idea of this workout is to force students to consciously make that switch—away from focusing on their own experience of past events and toward thinking about how to make those events meaningful, interesting, and relevant to the reader.

Directions

This workout is divided into three steps. Step 1 is a writing "trap." Its purpose is to allow students to fall into the trap of self-focus as they describe a past traumatic injury moment. Through discussion and writing, step 2 shifts their focus onto the experience they are creating for the reader. Step 3 is, then, their resulting story version to compare with that produced during step 1.

From *Writing Workouts to Develop Common Core Writing Skills: Step-by-Step Exercises, Activities, and Tips for Student Success, Grades 7–12* by Kendall Haven. Santa Barbara, CA: Libraries Unlimited. Copyright © 2015.

Step 1

The actual assignment for step 1 is intentionally vague.

Assignment: *Think of a time you were seriously hurt or injured and write about it. Describe what happened, what you were doing, and how you were injured/hurt.*

If any students claim to have never suffered any major injury or hurt, tell them to use the most serious injury that they can remember—even if it was only a splinter or a bee sting.

Have student write for 10 minutes.

Watch as they begin this 10-minute writing block, and note how many begin to write right away, how many pause to think and plan, and how many of those actually jot down any notes.

Step 2

Stop the writing and ask if everyone paused to plan the Eight Essential Elements before they began to write. (You will know from your observations exactly how many actually did.)

If the majority did not, have students formally write down main character, two relevant traits for this story, their story goal (what they were trying to do when they were injured, and why they were there), a motive (why that was important for them to do, and why they were doing that in the first place), and any problems and/or conflicts that they had to overcome.

Now lead a short discussion through these important questions:

- What is the *point* of this story?
- What will a reader think is the point of this story *for them*?
- What should the reader *take away* from it and remember?
- Why will a reader value reading about your experience?
- How will the reader be better off for having read this story?

For many students, these will be new concepts. Tell them that no writer can be successful and effective if their readers don't perceive exactly how the story relates to them and how it has meaning for them, the readers.

Have students write a one-sentence summary of the *central theme* of their story—what they want the reader to take away from the story and remember.

Allow several students to read their sentence and discuss as a class. Is that a reader-centric statement of the value of their story? If not, how could that sentence be reworded?

Step 3

Have students rewrite their story organizing it around the one-sentence takeaway theme they just wrote. That won't change the events, the characters, their goals and motives, or their actions. But it will change the way the student develops, presents, and describes these story elements.

Post-Activity Review and Discussion

Review the importance of thinking and planning from the audience's viewpoint (rather than from the author's). (I have included an extended section on this topic in my book *Story Smart*.)

Allow several students to read both versions of their injury story and compare as a class. Which drew you in more? Why?

Think of other stories and essays the class has read, and discuss how those authors worked to make their writing relevant to their intended audience.

Workout #12: Bored!

Quick Summary & Purpose

** **Purpose**: • Learn to more precisely and articulately describe character emotions and how those emotions affect perception.

Summary: It is always difficult for students to focus on a single emotion and describe it so well that readers acutely and vividly experience that same emotional feeling. Using boredom for that target emotion has several advantages: it's fun for students and, because its outward manifestations are relatively subtle, it requires more thought and care in crafting their description than other, more demonstrative, emotions would.

Key Grades

Best for middle school grades. Very good for high school

Time Required

Writing: 20 to 30 minutes
Review and discussion: 15 to 30 minutes
Revision & editing (optional): 20 to 30 minutes

Introduction

Every student claims to be bored much (if not most) of the time. Great! Let's use their intimate firsthand knowledge as the springboard for effective detail writing. In this workout they will describe "ultimate boredom." The idea is to push their description so that it oozes total boredom from every word. You can do this workout with and for any individual emotion. However, boredom is particularly good to use. I have found that more students are more eager to write about being bored than about any other emotion. It is also true that, if you can successfully radiate boredom in your writing, you can handily describe any other emotion.

Directions

It is a simple, straightforward assignment:

Assignment: *Think of a time you were really (REALLY) bored (B-O-R-E-D!) and describe both the feeling and that moment.*

From *Writing Workouts to Develop Common Core Writing Skills: Step-by-Step Exercises, Activities, and Tips for Student Success, Grades 7–12* by Kendall Haven. Santa Barbara, CA: Libraries Unlimited. Copyright © 2015.

Rules:

1. Students will write their description in first person.

2. Don't worry about length. Focus just on the power and effectiveness of your description

3. Your goal is to have everyone in the class agree that your description is the best representation of "ultimate boredom."

As writing hints and guides, tell students to concentrate on every nuance of what it feels like to be bored to death. How does it affect your perceptions? Your thinking? What do you do? What do you think? How does ultimate boredom affect you? Keep TIP #8: (TFSS) in mind while you write.

The key to success here are sensory details and internal thought details that pull the reader into the mind and feelings of the writer.

As an example:

Bad (telling, not showing): *I'm soooo bored. It's 2:30 and I'm still bored. Everything is boring.*

Better (show rather than tell): *2:06! 2:06!?! It's been an hour since 2:05! . . . Gravity is sucking me down like a blob into my chair. My hair grows heavy. Each heartbeat lasts for minutes. My mind is trapped in a gravity well dungeon being slowly tortured to death, killed by tiny pinpricks, screaming for escape. pricking my mind jab after jab and my arms are frozen by sledgehammer gravity. I can't stand these hours of endless torture. Aaauugh! Still 2:06! No! It must be the next day. Centuries have passed since 2:05. My eyelids are succumbing to the wretched pull of black-hole gravity. . . . A fly drones by, snail slow. It barely moves. I see each beat of its tiny wings. Each second has been shattered into a thousand broken pieces, each piece lasting longer than an hour. . . . Ha! 2:07! Only 53 minutes to the 3:00 bell. . . . I'll never survive. There is no world outside the endless tunnel of this minute. . . .*

Post-Activity Review and Discussion

Read all papers overnight and select six to be read to the class by the author. Alternately, have five or six volunteers read their description. After these readings, the class votes for the best description of "ultimate boredom."

Lead a class discussion on why that one description won the vote. What worked? What didn't? Require that students use specific wording for the read descriptions as their examples. Get you students to explore the breadth and depth of ways to communicate an emotion.

Finally (optional), have students rewrite their own descriptions and try to crank up the impact and emotional power of their writing.

Workout #13: The Ant Hill

Quick Summary & Purpose

** **Purpose**: • Learn to expand their thinking when describing events and activities in order to more fully communicate a central theme and idea to readers.

Summary: The question on the table with this workout is: how do you structure your written descriptions so as to impress readers with the complexity and level of effort required for an event? In this workout, students will experiment with the writing tools that create time-based suspense and excitement by describing the many individual efforts required to accomplish a single event. This will be a big writing assignment, one that typically requires both in-class and out-of-class writing effort.

Key Grades

Excellent for all grades

Time Required

Initial discussion: 40 to 45 minutes
Individual research and planning: 2 days
Writing: 45 minutes in-class plus a weekend for home writing
Review and discussion: one period

Introduction

Any substantial event is really the culmination of hundreds of small, individual events and efforts. Students tend to stay at the grand overview level in their descriptions—and thereby forego the writing power, suspense, excitement, and tension of drawing readers down in to the detailed trenches of the action.

Directions

For this workout, students will describe in minute detail a single, complex event. A good one to use is: preparing their school for opening day after summer break. Any complex, multifaceted event will do. That assignment, however, is one that is somewhat familiar and totally accessible to all students.

I like to begin this activity by reading a description by a grand master of such writing (James Michener) from his story "Alligator" in his book *Tales of the South Pacific*. That story certainly provides a powerful and graphic example of detailed event description. However, this is not the only example of effective preparatory storytelling. Showing clips of the reality show *Cupcake*

Wars, as an example, would be a good way to show the tension that builds up when preparing for something big.

I lead this assignment in four steps over the course of a week.

Tell students of this assignment and read the Michener story I mentioned (or other similar story of your choosing) as an example. Then lead a discussion with the class about the individual efforts required to get the school ready for opening day. Help them expand their thinking and the kinds of prep work required of the vast variety of groups (teachers, administrators, grounds keepers, supply, food service, bussing, crossing guards, etc.).

Now give students their actual writing assignment.

Assignment: *Write about the vast and complex effort to get the school ready for opening day.*

   Writing Requirements: Their written description must be:

- Specific and detailed
- As comprehensive as possible
- Exciting
- Filled with tension and suspense

Lead a discussion on a few of the writing tools they can use to accomplish those requirements.

- Put a face on it. (Identify and describe the characters responsible for each individual effort, and know their concerns and worries.)
- Time crunch. Use time as an organizing principle and as a source of building tension. ("Will they get it all done in time?!?")
- Problems and conflict. Insert as many problems and conflicts into individual efforts as you can. Obstacles create excitement and give you something to describe and to develop in your writing.
- Interweave individual efforts. Suspense and tension can come for the rapid jumps between individual efforts as they all try to meet the time deadlines.
- Short, choppy sentences add a sense of frantic and chaotic effort. (something to use at those moments of the greatest activity and stress).

Have students start a list of all possible sub-activities that contribute to the greater event of "getting the school ready for opening day." You can start this as a class discussion or turn it over to students as an individual effort. I prefer launching the assignment through a group discussion.

Send students out with a two-day assignment: get ready to write. That means they will have to complete their list of individual efforts, put names and descriptions to each, identify problems and conflicts, and decide on how they will count down to school opening. (Who does each job? What's involved? What are their problems and difficulties?)

This is the research phase. Encourage students to go talk to people in each position to find out what's involved.

Now they write their descriptions. I recommend that you start this writing in class (45 minutes) and then assign it as a weekend writing assignment thereafter. These will be substantial pieces and deserve to be given sufficient time for the writing.

Post-Activity Review and Discussion

Have a few students read their essay and then discuss as a class. What makes for vivid and compelling (engaging, impressive) event description? Five key writing tools should bubble to the top of this discussion:

- **Details.** Precise, specific, vivid details create the mental images that readers require.
- **Characters.** Characters lie at the heart of all effective writing. Give readers just enough so that they come to care about the characters and they will always care about the events and struggles of those characters.
- **Pacing.** If the action seems to happen rapid-fire and to jump from person to person and task to task, it creates a sense of urgency and suspense. Writing hint: Short, choppy sentences create the feeling of a faster pace and of more frantic action.
- **Time.** One of the best sources of narrative tension are time constraints. Time constraints create tension and excitement. The less time available and the more that must be done, the greater that tension and reader excitement.
- **Struggles.** If characters exert great effort in the face of significant problems and conflicts, it engages readers and holds their attention.

Workout #14: What Did You Have for Dinner?

Quick Summary & Purpose

** Purpose: • Develop a feel for using physical description to reveal character attitude and emotion.

Summary: At the heart of effective writing is the ability to convey character feelings, emotions, and reactions. This is the origin of the classic writing advice "Show, don't tell." Yet "showing" a character's emotional swings and reactions is a most advanced writing concept. This workout helps to develop that critical skill.

Key Grades

Excellent for all grades.

Time Required

Oral activity: 10 minutes
Review and discussion: 15 minutes
Written exercise: 30 to 40 minutes
Review and discussion: 20 to 45 minutes

Introduction

Writers need to be able to make readers interested in their characters (be they nonfiction or fiction). A large part of that task is accomplished by making readers feel that they "know" the characters. In the simplest terms, that means to make readers believe that they know how characters will feel, think, and react to new situations. How does a writer accomplish that? By showing readers how the character feels, thinks, reacts, and acts in several initial situations. This workout forces students to do exactly that.

Directions

Oral Activity

Each student must choose a partner and find out what that partner *actually* had for dinner last night. Give students a minute or two to complete this exchange. Now group students into groups of six. (Groups of five or seven will do if that makes the groups come out even.) It is preferable, but not essential, for partners to be in the same group.

Number the students in each group (1 through 6). Arbitrarily pick one number and have that numbered student in each group describe, in one minute, the meal told to him by his partner *as if it were the teller's favorite meal in all the world.* This teller may not alter the content of

From *Writing Workouts to Develop Common Core Writing Skills: Step-by-Step Exercises, Activities, and Tips for Student Success, Grades 7–12* by Kendall Haven. Santa Barbara, CA: Libraries Unlimited. Copyright © 2015.

the meal. His goal is to convince every person in the group that this is a truly delightful meal fit for their next special party or occasion.

After these students have finished, pick a second numbered student who will describe the meal described to her by her partner as if it were the worst excuse for food in the history of civilized dining, as if she wouldn't serve this slop to a cockroach. Again, the teller may not alter the content of the meal. This teller's goal is to turn the stomach of each listener with *how* she tells her description of this meal.

Finally, pick a third numbered student in each group to describe the meal told to him by his partner as if the individual elements of the meal were all right, but they made for a terrible combination. (Peanut butter and corn flakes are both fine—but not together!)

Feel free to change the assigned attitude of each teller to ones that you think would better match the interest and abilities of your students. It is, however, critically important that each teller be given an assigned attitude and motivation for their telling.

Review and Discussion

Following these three tellings, launch a class discussion with two question areas. Make a list of the valid responses from the class.

1. Did you see the assigned emotion? How did the tellers make you see it? This list should include as a minimum:
    - sensory detail (have students recall specific examples for various senses)
    - description of the setting
    - facial expression
    - gestures
    - tone of voice (along with volume and pace)
    - physical actions
    - similes (and other forms of analogy and comparison)

2. What made it fun? What held your attention? When did a teller lose your attention? This list should include as a minimum:
    - emotion
    - energy
    - expression
    - exaggeration
    - overreaction

These lists represent powerful writing tools for every student writer to practice and master in improving their character-based writing skill.

Written Exercise

Having experienced this exercise orally (the easy way to do it), and having created at least a partial list of the writing tools that can perform the same thing on paper, it's time for students to see what they can do as writers.

Give them a situational assignment. Here is one I often use.

Situation: Your grandmother gives you a sweater for your birthday. Your parents say that you have to wear it when granny comes to visit tonight. You are wearing the sweater and showing it to two of your good friends.

Assignment: Write two passages providing detailed descriptions of this conversation.

First passage: Write as if you think this is the ugliest, most embarrassingly horrid piece of clothing you have ever seen.

Second passage: Write as if you love this sweater so much you don't even mind that it doesn't fit. It's your new all-time favorite.

Each of these passages must be a minimum of a half page; max of one full page single spaced.

They will write the first passage in first person (as if they are now writing about their own previous experience). They will write the second passage in third person (as if this event is part of a story they are writing about a story character).

Before students begin to write, they should take a minute to make two decisions:

1. What is the relationship between the main character and the grandmother?
2. What is the voice and core personality for the main character?

Both of these choices should be clear to readers from how the two passages are written.

Finally, have students consider the two lists they created after the oral version of this workout. How will they employ those same tools in their writing?

Post-Activity Review and Discussion

Allow several students to read their two passages. Then hold a final workout discussion.

• Which passage was easier to write? It is most often easier to write this sort of passage in first person, and it is always easier to write about problems (things going wrong) than when everything is grand and happy.

• Was it easier to write about yourself or about a different character? Why?

Workout #15: The 30-Second Story

Quick Summary & Purpose

** **Purpose**: • Get students used to creating essential story elements.
　　　　　　　 • Teach students to search for and to recognize those same elements.

Summary: This is a fun and powerful oral game. It is flexible enough to teach any aspect of story planning and writing that you want to focus your class on. It engages the entire class. And it is delightfully fun for all.

Key Grades

Excellent for all grades.

Time Required

20 minutes per use

Introduction

This is one of those effective story-planning games that you can use over and over. It gets better as the students get better able to handle more complex assignments.

Having students actually write and present whole stories is very time consuming and stressful. It is a slow, labor-intensive way to develop writing skills. It is often far more productive to use an exercise where the class as a whole can focus on a specific problem area (e.g., description, character development, word choice, using multiple senses, etc.) still within the context of a story. The "30-Second Story" is one of the two most powerful story-writing or storytelling exercises I have ever developed, and one that allows your whole class to quickly and efficiently focus on any specific story concept or technique.

Directions

Bring four students to the front of the room and tell them that they are going to make up a four-minute story, 30 seconds at a time. While this is a verbal exercise, it focuses on aspects of story creation, structure, and development.

One student starts the story and tells for 30 seconds. Then the second, third, and fourth tellers each tell for 30 seconds. Now the first teller invents and tells the story for a second 30 seconds, and so forth to the fourth teller's second turn, during which time the story must be ended. You time each segment, calling, "Switch!" at the 30-second break points. There are no pauses for thought between tellers. The second one ends, the next begins, even if the story is in the middle of a sentence.

The *General Rules* keep this story from degenerating into a mindless, boring story, as most circle stories quickly become. The *Special Requirements* focus the class on whatever aspect of story and writing you want them to work on that day.

General Rules

These six rules apply every time your class uses the 30-Second Story workout. They should be considered a mandatory part of this exercise since they force the four students to create a single, unified story.

1. The first student starts the story by providing three key story elements during his/her first 30-second telling: identity of the main character, that character's goal during the story (what he or she wants to do or get), and an initial setting for the story.

2. The second teller, during their first 30-second telling, must create at least one suitable obstacle that blocks the main character from his or her goal. If the first teller provided one obstacle, the second provides a second obstacle.

3. Every teller must accept the first teller's main character and goal and use them as the focus and purpose for each story segment.

4. Every teller must pick up the story *exactly* where the previous teller stopped with no temporal or spatial jumps. They may not shift to other characters, other settings, or other events at the beginning of their 30-second period.

5. Any teller may resolve an obstacle, but must immediately pose another one to take its place, so that there is always at least one obstacle on the table for the character to struggle against.

6. The final teller must bring the story (goal of the main character) to some resolution during his or her final 30-second telling.

The class must track and evaluate each of the four students' success with each of the General Rules. This task helps every student recognize and appreciate the role of goal, conflict, and struggles in basic story structure.

Special Requirements

In addition to the *General Rules*, you will create *Special Requirements* for each telling. *Special Requirements* apply only to the current round of the 30-Second Story. After meeting these requirements under the pressure of a timed, improvised story in front of the class, students will find it easy to consider that facet of story writing in the future. You select the *Special Requirements* to emphasize and focus on any aspect of story writing you want the class to study.

Some commonly used *Special Requirements* are:

*   **Character Development.** Require that each teller reveal two new bits of significant information about the main character's history, likes, flaws, quirks, fears, physical presence, personality, activity, etc. during each of the teller's two 30-second telling periods.

- **Senses.** We often describe only what we see. Richer stories come from engaging more of the listener's senses. Require that each teller include detailed information about three, four, or all five senses during each 30-second telling.

- **Action Verbs.** Verbs of state (verbs such as is, are, was, am, were, etc. that only indicate a state of being) do little to fire a listener's imagination and create vivid, detailed mental images. Require that each teller use no more than two—or even one—verb of state in each telling.

  These verbs of state are often used as "helper" verbs. (He is going, or she was sitting.) Still they always pull energy out of the text compared to the simple tenses. (He goes. She sat.) Have the class keep track.

- **Passive Voice.** Using passive voice is another way to suck energy and excitement out of a text. ("The chair was placed at the table," as opposed to "Dave placed the chair at the table." "The data were shown to be significant," as opposed to "Sharon showed that the data were significant.") For that reason, there are times when it is useful. However, passive voice is (generally) overused, and used at many of the wrong places. Require that students use NO passive voice in any of their 30-second telling periods.

- **Descriptive Detail.** We all drop modifiers and write (or speak) in simple subject-verb sentences when we're not sure of what we're writing about. Hand each teller a slip of paper on which you have written an object with several appropriate modifiers (e.g., a long red string, or an empty brown bottle). Each teller will thus have their own object. During each of their two 30-second telling periods each teller must include that object with its modifiers in their story. The class's job is to detect what was written on each teller's paper. Each teller's job is to keep the class from successfully identifying the object. Tellers can succeed only by peppering their 30-second telling with other modifiers, thus disguising the ones assigned to them. Soon, searching for descriptive modifiers will be automatic.

- **Scene Description.** Young story writers often forget that, just because they can see each scene in their heads, readers cannot also see those scenes. Require that each teller spend half of his or her 30-second periods describing details of the scenes of the story.

Similarly, characterization, simile and metaphor, word choices, irony, or any other facet of story writing can become the Special Requirement focus of a 30-Second Story. As your students become more adept at the form of this exercise, you can give them two or three Special Requirements to accomplish during each telling session in addition to the General Rules.

Discuss with the class as a whole the four tellers' success with both General Rules and Special Requirements. Then discuss the effective use of, and importance of, the Special Requirements aspect of story construction. Finally, have a second group of four create a second story with the same Special Requirements. Have the class compare and contrast these two groups looking for improvement in the Special Requirements area.

In 20 minutes, two groups can create different stories while focusing on the *Special Requirement* of the day, and the whole class will have watched and discussed that aspect of story writing in some detail. If used only once a week, this technique will greatly expand your class's mastery of successful story structure.

Remember that making up a story under pressure, in front of peers, is much scarier than One-on-One-on-One-on-Ones or most other story-development exercises. Introduce the 30-Second Story without *Special Requirements*. Then gradually build into more complex requirements always keeping the tone that of a light-hearted game.

Options/Variations

Many teachers have found that their class responds more enthusiastically when a system of award points is created for the game. Tellers get points for successfully meeting General and Special Requirements. Class members get points for noting discrepancies, or for accurately tracking certain aspects of the Special Requirements. The race for points is on, and the class is hooked. They all wanted to be selected to the four-person story-creating team because tellers build more points. The audience studies every word, looking for points.

Post-Activity Review and Discussion

In any post-workout review and discussion, emphasize both the importance of the Special Requirement of the day and the central role of the General Rules in creating effective, successful stories. The General Rules represent the core layer of character information and the core of a story's structure.

Workout #16: Feeling the Feelin'

Quick Summary & Purpose

** **Purpose**: • Explore writing tools to communicate specific emotions and feelings to readers
   • An excellent demonstration of the "show, don't tell" concept.

Summary: "Show, don't tell," is one of the most frequently cited (and most overused) pieces of writing advice. This workout lets students experience the difference between "telling" and "showing" where it applies most directly and emphatically: with character development.

Key Grades

Excellent for all grades

Time Required

Step 1: 15 minutes
Step 2: 15 minutes
Step 3: 20 to 30 minutes
Step 4: 30 to 40 minutes

Introduction

This workout is a wonderful chance to develop two writing concepts. The first is a clear demonstration of the "show, don't tell" concept. That term applies most directly to the emotions and reactions of characters—which is the writing focus of this workout. Second, this workout allows students to explore how to effectively and powerfully describe a character's emotions and feelings so that readers vicariously feel (experience) the same feeling.

Secondarily, this four-step workout reinforces the power and necessity of planning (create first; write second).

Directions

Step 1.

This workout starts with a simple, straightforward writing assignment.

Assignment: *Think of a time you felt a strong emotion. Describe that event (or moment) so that the reader will clearly see and vicariously feel that same emotion.*

Have students write for 10 minutes.

From *Writing Workouts to Develop Common Core Writing Skills: Step-by-Step Exercises, Activities, and Tips for Student Success, Grades 7–12* by Kendall Haven.

72   Santa Barbara, CA: Libraries Unlimited. Copyright © 2015.

Step 2

Stop their writing and discuss:

- Was it easy or hard to write about this emotion and this moment so that readers would viscerally, vicariously feel the writer's emotion?
- Did students actually state the emotion ("tell it")? Have them underline the word (mad, sad, happy, afraid, scared, etc.) in their writing each time they did.
- What would it look like to "show" the same emotion (so that you wouldn't have to actually write—tell—it)? Pick one or two examples from student writing and have the class suggest how you would "show" the same emotion in the same situation—that is, show how the character reacts and what the character does, so that readers can correctly infer their emotion.
- Did each student pause to plan his or her story? Did they pause to define each of the Essential Elements?

Have students make a list of the following Essential Elements for each of the major characters in their story (themselves especially).

- Two interesting traits (Emphasis here should be on aspects of personality and attitude)
- Goal (What they were doing (or trying to do) just before they felt this strong emotion)
- Motives (Why it was important for each character to achieve this immediate goal)
- The key TFSS (see TIP #8—How does the main character think, feel, sense (or perceive) the setting and situation, and say details they will use to better show the emotions to readers?)

Step 3

Have students rewrite their story incorporating this additional information. Give them 20 to 30 minutes for this task.

Step 4

Now the fun part. Have each student decide what would be the *opposite* emotion of the one they actually felt in that situation.

Tell the class that you want them to *reverse* their (the main character's) emotional reaction to this situation. They will now rewrite their story so that the main character reacts in this opposite emotional way at the moment they felt that strong emotion. What (internally and situationally) would have to change to make those new emotions make sense?

Writing Rules:

1. Continue to write in first person (even though this is now technically fiction).
2. Use the same characters, same interactions between characters, same events, and the same locations and settings.

It's the same story shifted just enough to allow for the main character (the writer) to experience the opposite emotion that they described in steps 1 and 3.

Give them a bit more time for this writing. I usually allow 30 to 40 minutes

Post-Activity Review and Discussion

Compare the writing produced in steps 1, 3, and 4. Typically, the writing at step 3 is a strong improvement over that of step 1. Emphasize that this reinforces the value of planning—especially the character elements, TFSS details (especially the sensory details).

Compare the writing of steps 3 and 4. Step 3 is based on nonfiction experiences. Step 4 forces students to imagine the TFSS details for their main character. Yet students will have to infer and assume these details for most of the nonfiction writing they ever attempt and, certainly, for all of their fiction writing. It is a valuable writing tool to practice seeing the world through some other character's eyes.

Quick Summary & Purpose

** **Purpose:** • Teach deeper story comprehension skills.
   • Develop a better sense of, and appreciation for, the power of character motive as a determinant of reader reaction to, and feelings about, both the character and the story.

Summary: There is no better way to decide if a character's actions were right or wrong, justified or unjustified, than to hold a courtroom trial where students can present the arguments pro and con and debate the issue. Students love the courtroom drama and get a valuable opportunity to evaluate complex character behavior and its relationship to the students' own world.

Key Grades

Excellent for all grades

Time Required

To organize and assign roles: 20 to 30 minutes
Student planning time: 3 to 4 days elapsed time with no specific classroom time devoted to their work
Actual trial: 30 to 60 minutes
Post-activity Discussion: 20 minutes

Introduction

It is always clear whether or not a story character did it or didn't do it. The story text tells us. However, major questions often linger over whether or not that character was justified (morally or ethically) to do what they did—about whether they were "right" or "wrong" to do it. That analysis requires a deeper level of story understanding and tends to focus on character motive. That question is also the focus of this workout.

Directions

Pick a story and read it with the class. Best if the story is both familiar and short (folk tales are typically ideal). Pick a story in which characters do things that are technically a crime: "The Big Bad Wolf" (property destruction), "Goldilocks" (breaking and entering), "Wile E. Coyote" (attempted murder), etc.

You decide on the most appropriate character to "arrest" and charge with ***morally unjustifiable actions***. Notice that you will not hold court to decide if they "did it." That has already been established by the factual statements of the story. The trial will determine whether or not that character was justified in doing what he or she did. With only rare exception, this will be either the main character or the antagonist.

Announce to the class that they will hold a formal courtroom trial to judge the actions of this character and decide if the character you have chosen to arrest was justified or not. The class must agree on the specifics of the charges (which exact actions were unjustifiable and wrong). Reemphasize that the charge is not guilt or innocence (that's a factual question that was answered by story information), but were they *justified* in doing it (a moral and ethical question for students to debate).

Now pick students and appoint them as the principal positions for the trial. Pre-appoint the following positions:

1. **Judge.** The judge is responsible for procedural matters (allowing questions to be asked, handling objections, allowing witnesses to be called, etc.) and ensuring that no direct story information is contradicted by any witness. (In some classrooms the teacher holds this position herself.)

2. **Prosecutor(s).** Prosecutors must identify all information in the story that tends to incriminate the defendant (show that the defendant's actions are not justifiable) and to identify the story witnesses who could best report that information during the trial. Witnesses need not have appeared in the actual story, but must have a strong reason to know firsthand the information they will report. Additional background and character witnesses may also be created and called.

3. **Defense Counsel(s).** Defense counsel must prepare *for* the defendant what the prosecutor is trying to prepare *against* them.

4. **Defendant.** The defendant must be thoroughly familiar with the story and prepare, with defense counsel, explanations to rationalize and justify their reported story actions.

Other witnesses will be selected from the class membership as needed by either team of lawyers. The rest of the class will act as jury.

Allow two or three days for each team of lawyers to build their case and decide on a list of witnesses. (Many of those witnesses will not have appeared in the original story but will either be outside character witnesses or unreported witnesses to story events.) Witness lists must then be submitted to the judge and approved by both the judge and you. You will probably want to limit the number of witnesses each side may call.

Regularly consult with the two teams of attorneys to make sure that they each have a good story line for their case and have developed it sufficiently to have specific witnesses and a list of specific questions for each. Encourage them to think creatively in what they will try to prove in court and in how they will solicit the needed information from witnesses.

Lawyers may definitely bring in information, witnesses, ideas that are not in the original story. Help them make the trial fun for the class as well as instructive about the power of motives. Help the lawyer teams explore the motives of the defendant (*why* they did what they did) and also how they will bring that information into the trial.

Even if you have appointed a student judge, you will serve as the ultimate story defendant: overrule anything that factually violates the story.

Assign the role of each approved witness to different students who should have enough time to review the story and decide what they would and wouldn't logically know, how they feel about story events, and to infer any history they need to explain their position and their interpretation of story events. Each witness (in collaboration with the lawyer team that will bring them into court) is free to add anything not directly covered in the story. But they cannot contradict the actual, stated story without your express permission.

On the day of the trial, physically set up the classroom as a courtroom. The judge can swear in the witnesses before they testify.

Hold the trial: defense case first; prosecution second. Don't have the jury deliberate after the trial. Simply have them vote to see who won.

Post-Activity Review and Discussion

Good stories often place characters in the kind of jeopardy that requires them to make shaky moral and ethical decisions. This is the perfect fodder for a character trial.

There is no factual issue at stake in the trial. Story information establishes the guilt of the defendant. Being justified in a technically illegal act, however, is a moral and ethical question. These questions require us to know the defendant better, to understand his or her motives and feelings.

At the end of the trial, regardless of the outcome, the story and story characters will be more interesting and more important to your students. Character information creates a sense of closeness. The more often students experience that concept, the more likely they are to fully develop the characters they tell or write about.

Workout #18: Progressive Stories

Quick Summary & Purpose

** **Purpose:** • Reinforce student awareness of the essential structural elements of effective stories.

Summary: This is another in the series of quick, in-class story development workouts that develop student confidence in their use of, and mastery of, the Eight Essential Elements of effective narrative writing.

Key Grades

Excellent for all grades

Time Required

15 minutes (oral)
30 minutes (written)

Introduction

In this version of the classic progressive story, each student writes their additions to each building story, rather than sharing them orally.

Directions

The general rules for a written progressive story are that each student will add to the story they receive for a fixed amount of time (generally 30 to 60 seconds) during each time period and then pass the story on to another student. Depending on the format you choose, you will have to allot some additional time for each new student to read the existing story before that student's writing time begins.

The general rules are:

1. Each student must start his or her additions *exactly* where the previous student left the story.

2. No temporal ("and in 50 years . . .") or spatial ("and across the globe in Australia . . .") jumps are allowed.

3. Each student must keep the same main character goal that was initially established.

4. If a student solves a problem, he must replace it with another problem or conflict so that the next writer will have something given to him to write about.

From *Writing Workouts to Develop Common Core Writing Skills: Step-by-Step Exercises, Activities, and Tips for Student Success, Grades 7–12* by Kendall Haven. Santa Barbara, CA: Libraries Unlimited. Copyright © 2015.

I have tried two options for this version of the progressive story:

1. Two students partner. Each starts a story, and then these two students pass their two stories back and forth between them, each adding to these same two stories on each pass.

   The advantage here is that each student is familiar with both stories and requires less reading time to be ready to write the next addition to it. If you allow each student to write for 30 seconds and to read for 30 seconds, they will always have plenty of time for the reading no matter how long the total story becomes.

   The one potential problem with this scheme is that strong disagreements often arise over the direction and development of one or both of the stories, and the two students become frustrated.

2. Each story passes, student by student, around the room as each new student adds his or her contribution.

   A potential time problem emerges with this scheme. After three or four students have written their parts to the story, you must allow longer and longer reading blocks before each new student begins to write. I generally start this reading time at 15 seconds and then add 10 to 15 seconds for each extra segment the student must read and absorb before writing.

   It is also essential for this option to place additional requirements on each new writer. The first student must create a main character and a goal. The second must create a problem or conflict that blocks the main character from goal attainment. Each new student can only solve an existing problem if he or she also creates a new problem. Each new contributor must include one new bit of character information (trait) for others to use. . . . That sort of thing.

Optional Rules

You may assign additional requirements to each student as they write each contribution to these progressive stories. The most common are these: (I recommend that you pick no more than two of these additional writing requirements. Just keeping the story line going is hard enough.)

Each time a student contributes new writing to a story, she must:

- Include one new piece of character Information about the main character.
- In some way increase the risk and/or danger the main character faces.
- Include two bits of sensory detail (not both from the same sensory organ).
- Reveal an additional motive for the main character.

Post-Activity Review and Discussion

No post-activity discussion is necessary. Do it as a fun activity and move on with the day. The learning comes from how students plan and ponder their contributions to each progressive story.

Workout #19: Interrupter

Quick Summary & Purpose

** **Purpose**: • Students learn the value of, and contribution of, both sides of the brain to creating engaging stories.

Summary: This is a short oral game-format activity that dramatically demonstrates the separation of factual/plot-based story information from story energy and emotion both in the mind of the creator and in the mind of the story listener—and the importance of creating blended and balanced contributions from both in effective narratives of any style and genre.

Key Grades

Excellent for all grades

Time Required

15 minutes for the oral game
10 to 15 minutes for analysis and discussion

Introduction

Kindergartners create rambling stories that go nowhere but are filled with infectious, enticing energy and passion. Middle-schoolers write with plot-conscious precision, but tend toward emotionless tedium. We need both elements in our stories: logical plot flow and infectious energy. But they come from different parts of the brain. Here's a fun workout to demonstrate that distinction and to help students develop the ability to incorporate both sides into their planning and writing.

Directions

Every student in the class needs a partner. Partners must sit as close as possible since it will get raucously noisy and they need to hear each other. Partners agree on who is #1 and who is #2. Person #1 is designated as the **Storyteller**. Her job is to improvisationally create and tell a one-minute, fictional story to her partner.

Person #2 is designated not as the listener, but as the **Interrupter**. The Interrupter's job is to regularly interrupt the Storyteller by blurting out any random word that crosses his mind. It's better if the word has absolutely no connection to the story being told.

The Storyteller *MUST* incorporate each blurted word into the next sentence of her story. The Storyteller may not refuse a word or pretend not to hear. They must listen for, accept, and use every word the Interrupter blurts.

From *Writing Workouts to Develop Common Core Writing Skills: Step-by-Step Exercises, Activities, and Tips for Student Success, Grades 7–12* by Kendall Haven. Santa Barbara, CA: Libraries Unlimited. Copyright © 2015.

The Interrupter must interrupt at regular, frequent intervals. As a general guide, as soon as the Storyteller has completed the sentence incorporating one word into the story, the Interrupter should blurt out another.

What does it sound like? Here is a quick, typical sample of this joint creative process. ST designates lines by the Storyteller. I is for the Interrupter.

ST: A cat leapt onto the alley fence.

I: Pajamas.

ST: A man wearing pajamas yelled at the cat from an upstairs window . . .

I: Peanut butter.

ST: To go eat some peanut butter instead of howling.

I: Shark.

ST But the cat couldn't because a shark was guarding the grocery store.

Time these stories for one minute. There will be lots of noise and laughter. These stories are outrageously fun. Stopping them will require an attention-getting noise maker. A coach's whistle has always been my favorite.

Have partners reverse roles and start a completely new story so that everyone gets to experience both sides of this exercise. Again, time this new story for one minute.

Lead a brief discussion about their reactions to this experience. Which was harder, telling or interrupting? Which was more fun? (Typically a class will split pretty evenly on their answers to these questions.) Were the stories fun? (Universally they'll answer, "yes.") Did they create any good stories they want to share with the class? (Typically, "no.") Did their stories have strong character development? Clearly defined goal and motives? Powerful obstacles and antagonists? (Always the answer is "no.") But they were fun? ("Yes!")

Announce that you want to repeat the exercise but feel you need to adjust one little rule. The Storyteller's job will remain exactly the same as before. The Interrupter will interrupt at the same rate as before. But, instead of interrupting with some fiendishly random word, they *must*, at every interruption, feed to the Storyteller the ***"perfect word for them to use to keep the story going where it's going and make it better."*** (I have found that that exact wording is important. Best if you repeat it a time or two so that it truly sinks in.)

After all, the Storyteller has to create all the words. The Interrupter only has to create one word for every sentence or two. So that one word should be ***the perfect word to make this a truly great story***.

Again the Storyteller may not reject any word the Interrupter provides. The Interrupter may not pass, saying either that he couldn't think of a word or that the Storyteller was doing just fine without them. Interrupters must do their part and interrupt at the same rate as before. All that has changed is the Interrupter's goal in selecting words with which to interrupt the story.

Do two one-minute stories so that both students experience both roles. Now repeat the discussion and compare this experience to the first story. You will notice right away that the room is quieter during this second set of stories.

Was it easier or harder to be the Storyteller this time? Was it easier or harder to be the Interrupter? Were the stories more or less fun? (Most will answer, "Less.") Did they have a more understandable plot structure? (Typically yes.) Were the characters better defined? (Typically yes.) Were they better stories? (Typically mixed answer. Being fun is part of what makes a story good.)

Post-Activity Review and Discussion

Now the point of the exercise. What you and your students have just demonstrated is the difference between left-brained and right-brained thinking. The first story was pure right-brained fun. Everyone intuitively understands that the story will be a nonsense story. Their job is to pour as much fun, farce, energy, and enthusiasm into it as possible.

Because of the rule change, everyone feels responsible for creating a "real story" during the second round. Often the interrupted words are no better, and no more helpful, than on the first round. But now everyone treats them differently. This feeling of responsibility shifts participant thinking to logical, structural, left-brained thinking. Everyone thinks in terms of plot flow, cause-effect sequencing, rational plausibility, and logical structure. Fun is forgotten.

For a story to work, it needs both sides. Every writer is more comfortable working on one side of their brain or the other. The trick is to incorporate that side you are less comfortable with.

The left side provides order, logic, plot, structure. The right side provides energy, passion, humor, fancy, exaggeration. The left side creates core character information. The right side creates characterization. The left side tells us WHAT. The right side tells us HOW.

Writers need to successfully involve both sides in their stories.

Workout #20: One-on-One-on-One-on-One

Quick Summary & Purpose

** **Purpose**: • Demonstrate and teach an extremely powerful and effective planning tool for all forms and genre of writing.

Summary: This is a fast oral exercise that accomplishes an amazing amount of story (narrative) development and planning over a brief time period.

Key Grades

Excellent for all grades.

Time Required

Less than 15 minutes plus any additional time you want to allow for note taking.

Introduction

We refine story elements best with feedback. Most writers, however, work in isolation devoid of outside help. What could be more constructive, then, than trying some story structure and presentation; receiving instant, detailed feedback; and after a moment of reflection, getting to revise the material and try it again? That is the idea of One-on-One-on-One-on-One.

Directions

This is the most powerful, efficient, and effective story-related exercise I have ever developed. It's easy to use and never fails to improve both the writing at hand and the student's understanding of the form and structure of effective narratives. It is an oral exercise.

First assign a story topic for this exercise. If this exercise and topic are being used as part of the development of an existing story, no lead time is necessary. Announce the topic and launch into the exercise. Normally, these topics relate to specific aspects of a story you want your students to further develop (e.g., tell about the main character, about the character's struggles and problems, about the antagonist, or about the story line itself).

If this exercise is being used to develop student awareness of how to shape, organize, and deliver effective stories, announce the topic several days ahead of time. You *can* use fictional topics, but it is better to start with factual events students recall from their own lives. Keep the topics simple and personal so that the stories will be easy to recall and hold in their minds while they tell and then revise their story.

From *Writing Workouts to Develop Common Core Writing Skills: Step-by-Step Exercises, Activities, and Tips for Student Success, Grades 7–12* by Kendall Haven. Santa Barbara, CA: Libraries Unlimited. Copyright © 2015.

Any readily available topic will do: something that happened on a summer vacation trip, some time when you got in trouble, something that happened on a bike, something that happened on the school playground, someone who gave you something very special, someone who has been especially important to you, etc. Tell the class that they will tell a one-minute story on that topic.

Have students pair off for the exercise itself. All telling will be done one-on-one. These pairs sit facing each other, knee-to-knee and eye-to-eye with no desks or tables between them. They quickly agree on who is "#1" and who is "#2." As soon as they are settled, you call, "Person number 1 begin your story." Person #1 tells her story (or describes her main character—depending on the topic you assigned) to person #2. Person #2 listens. There should be no interruptions, questions, or comments from listeners. Their feedback will all be nonverbal.

You time the story, shouting "Stop!" after one minute. Immediately you direct Person #2 to begin his story. Person #2 tells *his* story while person #1 listens. To avoid having to yell, some teachers use coach's whistles for start and stop signals. Don't allow any discussion time between stories. Make these transitions as rapid as possible.

As person #2 finishes his minute of telling, have everyone switch partners. Again allow for no discussion or comment time. As soon as they are settled with their new partner, they repeat the exercise. Finally, they switch partners again and each tells his or her story for a third and final time to this new (third) partner.

Many teachers vary the times for each telling in two ways. First, there is nothing magic about 60 seconds for the duration of each telling. Some teachers shorten the time to 45 seconds, slowly increasing that time toward one minute over the course of the school year. Others allow students to talk a little longer. I recommend that you never go longer than 90 seconds for each student's telling.

Second, many teachers trim a few seconds off the first telling and add a few onto the third round of tellings without announcing it to the class. Tell students each round will be a one-minute telling. Then actually stop them at 50 or 55 seconds the first time and at 70 seconds the third. Stories grow with practice. They'll need more time to tell the same story during the third round.

In less than 15 minutes a vast amount of telling, assessment, and critical listening have taken place. Each student has talked about some assigned aspect of his or her writing; seen in the faces of the listeners if it worked effectively; restructured, reworded, and revised that story twice based on the feedback received and the student's own impressions of the story; and tested the effectiveness of each of these revised versions through their second and third tellings. While listening, students provide real-time, nonverbal feedback through facial and body reactions for the teller to use. They are also mentally revising their own story, and are sifting through the structure and wording of the story they are listening to for any ideas and phraseology they want to borrow and incorporate into their own story.

Every student can do a One-on-One-on-One-on-One. No one is embarrassed or forced to struggle in front of the class. One-on-One-on-One-on-Ones greatly enhance confidence and enthusiasm. They build a solid sense of effective story structure, pacing, and delivery. They give students a chance to explore variations and options in the way they structure story material.

Options/Variations

Assigning a clear, manageable, specific topic is critical to One-on-One-on-One-on-One success. Four topics are most successful if this exercise is used as part of the story development process:

1. The Main Character: Who is this character and what makes him so fascinating and worthy of a story? This allows students to employ all layers of character description and all facets of core character information for their story to present an intriguing, compelling character.

2. Struggles and Conflicts: What are they and what makes the obstacles, conflicts, struggles, problems, and associated risk and danger in this story big enough and formidable enough to carry a story and engross a reader?

3. Story Line: How are they going to order and pace the events of their story to successfully lead the listener or reader?

4. The Antagonist. The antagonist is the embodiment of the problems and obstacles faced by the main character. The bigger, the more dangerous, the riskier the antagonist is, the better readers will like both the main character and the story.

After using One-on-One-on-One-on-One several times, many teachers follow the exercise with an evaluation period. Quick written critiques work better than class discussions. Have students make journal entries answering two groups of questions.

First:

- How did my story change between the three tellings and why?
- Did my story improve over the three tellings? Why or why not?
- How would I reorganize this material if I were to tell it again?

Second, of the three stories I heard:

- Which did I enjoy the most, and why?
- Which scene can I most vividly remember, and why?
- What did the teller do to make me remember it?
- When did I laugh? What did the teller say to make me laugh?
- When was I most bored, and why?
- What did the teller say to make me so bored?

These evaluations help students fix what they have learned about their story, and stories in general, in their mind. They also become a good reference list of how to make a story work. What worked *on* a student will work *for* that student. What bored them will bore others. You might keep these critiques on file as a good progress check on each student's writing development.

Post-Activity Review and Discussion

During a One-on-One-on-One-on-One, every student both works continuously on their own story and assists their partner in their effort. While students aren't actually telling their own story, they accomplish three important tasks. First, they provide instant, explicit, non-verbal feedback for the teller. Because they are in the teller's face, the teller can't avoid recording and interpreting this nonverbal feedback. Second, they review and restructure their own stories for the next telling. Third, they sift through the structure, phraseology, and wording of the teller's story for anything they want to borrow and incorporate into their own work.

This exercise is also an excellent opportunity to review what makes a story work—characters, goals, conflicts, struggles, risk and danger, jeopardy, character reactions, and detail. There are infinite variations in the ways to organize and present this material. Yet every successful story has those elements tightly woven into it.

Workout #21: Story Teams

Quick Summary & Purpose

** **Purpose**: • Make all students more consciously aware of the Eight Essential Elements (see TIP #5) and of their power and contribution to a story.

Summary: In any well-written narrative, the Eight Essential Elements blend into a seamless whole. This workout gives students repeated chances to search for, and tear out of the complete narrative fabric, individual elements to better understand and appreciate what each looks like and what each contributes to the whole.

Key Grades

Excellent 7th to 9th. Good 10th to 12th.

Time Required

20 to 30 minutes to establish teams
10 to 15 minutes when reporting

Introduction

In any well-written narrative, the Eight Essential Elements blend into a seamless whole —like the individual instruments in an orchestra, like the individual threads in a rich tapestry. It is difficult (at best) to isolate any one element and its contribution to the narrative—just as it is most difficult to pick out the contribution of the 2nd violin or the oboe in a full orchestral piece without special training.

Two ways around this problem: first, have students consciously build each essential element before they begin to write. Second, assign students to search for and to report on individual elements in published narratives that the class is exposed to. That is the idea for this workout.

Directions

Divide the class into Story Element teams, one for each of the first six of the Eight Essential Elements (see TIP #5 for this list). Each time the class creates any narrative, these teams must define and contribute whatever information is needed that is relevant to their assigned element.

Any time the class reads any published narrative, each team is required to dissect the piece and isolate those words and sentences that present part of their element and to report on them to the class. (Character trait information, for example, could be scattered throughout a short story— some of it overtly stated and some strongly implied. The Character Trait Team would have to locate and report on all of this information.)

From *Writing Workouts to Develop Common Core Writing Skills: Step-by-Step Exercises, Activities, and Tips for Student Success, Grades 7–12* by Kendall Haven. Santa Barbara, CA: Libraries Unlimited. Copyright © 2015.

87

You should periodically rotate students to new teams so that all students eventually have had to search for and isolate each of these six of the Eight Essential Elements.

NOTE: There is no team for Element #7, Struggles, because struggles represents the plotting events of the narrative and includes most scenes and all actions in the piece. Further, plot is dependent on character. Thus, analyzing the first six elements will reveal what has to happen during the plot.

Neither is there a Team for Element #8, Details, because virtually every word in a tight narrative is a detail describing character, setting, or event. (We create stories; we write details!)

Teams and Assigned Mandate

1. **Character Team.** Characters are those entities that occupy the major character positions in a story. The Character Team is responsible for identifying the position (or positions) held by each new character. When creating new characters, this team must identify species, name, and relative age as well as the character positions the character performs during the story.

   Here is a list of the major character positions in a narrative. See *Story Smart* for a complete explanation.

   - **Main Character** This is the character that the story is "about." It's "their story." Technically, the main character is that character whose primary goal is resolved at the resolution point of the story.
   - **Antagonist** The antagonist is the physical embodiment of the single greatest obstacle blocking the main character from reaching his/her goal. In the climax scene, the main character will confront this antagonist for the final time in this story.
   - **Climax Character** At the climax moment of the story, *someone* will act to create the final outcome of that climax and define how the story will resolve. That character is often the Main Character, sometimes the Antagonist. But it doesn't have to be either of these two. In some stories a side character steps up to become the hero and "save the day," taking on the role of the western movie cavalry who always rode to the rescue just in the nick of time.

     Whoever steps up to assume this climax character role and determine the outcome of the story climax (and face its associated risks and dangers) becomes a central figure in defining the meaning and impact of the story for the audience.
   - **Authority Figure** Every story exists within some social structure or system (a school, a company, a club, an ecosystem, a family, a church, a kingdom, etc.), a system defined by lines of authority and by the rules that govern life within the system. Someone has to represent the authority of that system and wield that system's authority, responsibility, and power (ex.: teacher, king, manager, CEO, governor, parent, priest, sheriff, emperor, chief, top predator, etc.).
   - **Supporting Characters** Each of these characters can have supporters, helpers, or minions under them. These supporters are not, typically, considered to be major story characters.

- **Neutrals** Some characters exist in a narrative only to provide "local color" and background. These are characters that do not contribute to the major events, conflicts, or goals of the story.
- **Story Teller** This is the character who tells the story, the character through whose eyes we (readers/listeners) see the story (often called the Viewpoint Character).

2. **Character Trait Team.** Character traits are those bits of information about a character that make the character of interest to, and memorable to, readers. Effective character traits are specific, unusual, unique (point out how this character is different from others), and vivid (strong sensory information). Traits may either be overtly stated in a narrative or implied through the actions and interactions of a character.

   The Character Trait Team is responsible for identifying stated and strongly implied traits for all major story characters and for keeping a log of that information for other teams to use and refer to.

   There are many possible categories of character information. Literally, anything that differentiates one character from those around him/her can be used as an effective trait. As a starting guide, here are 13 categories of character trait information your students on this team should be aware of. There are many other categories (and many subcategories) they can add to this list as their skill at spotting and creating effective traits increases.

PHYSICAL	INTERNAL	SITUATIONAL
1. Name	7. Personality	13. Typical Reactions
2. Sensory Info	8. Voice (physically & emotionally)	
3. Job/Activity/	9. Abilities/Talents Quirks/Habits	
4. History	10. Weakness/Flaws	
5. Comparisons	11. Passions (Reminds You of?)	
6. Relationships	12. Fears	

3. **Goal Team.** A goal is a tangible, physical thing or discrete accomplishment that a character wants or needs to do or get in a story. It is the physical thing that drives the character; that the character is after. Often, characters have more than one goal at the same time. However, the story's main character always has one, primary goal—the goal that is resolved at the resolution point of the story.

   It is important that readers can readily and accurately visualize every goal.

   This team must identify the main character's primary goal and any secondary goals as well as the primary goals for every major character in the narrative.

4. **Motives Team.** Motives explain why a character's goal is important to the character. There can be many motives that help explain why a character needs to achieve that goal.

   Motives do not have to be physical, visualizable, tangible things. Love, hate, revenge, patriotism, pride, self-sacrifice, greed, etc.—these are powerful motives that explain why a character tries to do what he/she does. The key question for the Motive Team is: "*Why* do characters need to do or get what they are after?"

The Motive Team must discern all stated and implied motives for every identified goal for each of the major characters in a narrative and report them to the other teams.

5. **Problems & Conflicts Team.** Problems and conflicts include anything and everything (anyone and everyone) that blocks or prevents a character from achieving a stated goal(s). Anything could become a story problem or conflict if it serves to block (even temporarily) a character's progress toward a goal.

   The Problem & Conflict Team must identify and name each and every problem and conflict affecting the major story character, and must label it as either a problem or a conflict. (Conflict is a subset of problem that places one character in direct opposition to another character or entity in the story.)

6. **Risk & Danger Team.** Risk is the likelihood that something will go wrong. Danger is a measure of what (bad) could happen if things do go wrong. Problems and conflicts create risk and danger for a character.

   As the class progresses through a story, the Risk & Danger Team must identity all stated and apparent dangers and risks (the probability that the dangers will be individually or collectively realized). This team must constantly ask, "What could go wrong? What is the worst thing that could happen? How likely is each of those catastrophes?"

   The Risk and Danger Team must be ready to itemize the risk and danger facing each of the major characters.

Using Story Element Teams

There are two ways to use Story Element Teams

1. **When the class creates new stories.** Try creating a class story using the teams to create the essential elements. Start with Character Team, which creates the Main Character. The Character Trait Team then creates two or three interesting traits for this character. The Goal Team defines the principle (and any secondary) goals for this character. The Motive Team must explain why that principal goal is critically important to the main character.

   If, during their presentations, either of these teams mentions a new character, their presentation is temporarily halted while the Character Team must identify this new character and the major position (if any) that this character fills in the story. The Trait Team must then create two interesting traits for this new character, and the Goal Team must decide what this new character is after in the story.

   When the Problem & Conflict Team identifies an antagonist, their presentation is temporarily halted while this character is taken back to the Character Team for naming and definition, to the Trait Teams for characterization, and to the Goal and Motive Teams to define the driving forces behind this character.

As each team reports their contribution to the growing story, the other teams are free to challenge any offering—but only on two grounds:

1. The offered information is not strictly within the jurisdiction of that team.
2. The offered information contradicts information already presented and accepted by the class.

Any such challenges must be discussed and resolved before the team reporting can continue.

The game progresses in this way. Each time any team mentions new information that requires input from a previous team, pause and jump back for that team's input and work your way forward again. By the time the Risk & Danger Team (who have been tracking and assessing all information being created by the other teams) reports out to the class, you will always find that you have created a powerful, delightful, and compelling story . . . . Highly instructive and fun, too!

2. **When reading and analyzing existing narratives.** You periodically announce ahead of time when you want all story element teams to report. This typically is either at the end of a new short piece they have read or, periodically, as you work your way through a novel.

As each team reports, the class (other teams) must accept their presented information. Challenges should be limited to three areas.

1. The offered information is not strictly within the jurisdiction of that team.
2. The offered information contradicts information already presented and accepted by the class.
3. The team has failed to report some significant piece of information that is important to the story and that the team should have included in their presentation.

Any student making a challenge must provide specific reasons and evidence for their challenge. The class discusses, decides on the challenge, and adjusts the reported information if necessary.

Post-Activity Review and Discussion

No specific post-workout discussion is necessary. Teaching value is in the activity and in the periodic discussions along the way.

Workout #22: It Never Happened

Quick Summary & Purpose

** **Purpose**: • Develop skills for effectively writing events and for blending hypothetical events with descriptions of actual events.

Summary: It is far easier to write about things that happen than to write about things that don't. However, it is a valuable writing skill to be able to present hypothetical (or nonexistent) events with the same power and appeal as one presents actual events. That is the focus of this workout.

Key Grades

Excellent for all grades

Time Required

Initial discussion and definitions: 10 minutes
Writing: 45 to 60 minutes

Introduction

It's easy to describe things that happen. It is, however, far more difficult to make events that never happened seem as vivid, compelling, and real to readers as those that actually do. It is, of course, difficult to write about events that never happened since they . . . well . . . never happened. The design of this workout gives students a chance to wrestle with this writing tool.

Directions

This is a single-write assignment that needs minimal prep work and explanatory development. As worded here, it is a Christmas assignment. Because of most children's emotional attachments to, and expectations of, that day, it is a good choice. However, you can shift the assignment to other significant days/holidays if you prefer.

The assignment: *You will write an essay on "The Best Thing That Never Happened at Christmas."*

You will always get many repetitions of the "I don't get it!" and "What do you mean?" whines. You can, if you want, discuss what the assignment means. There are two possible interpretations:

1. Something that the student author is glad hasn't happened (that either had happened in past Christmases or that was regularly threatened to happen at Christmas)

2. Something that would have been the "best thing that could happen at Christmas"—but it never has

Either interpretation of this assignment is valid. You can discuss with them that this is a character essay, told purely from the point of view of the student author.

The Rules:

1. The essays will be written in first person.

2. The student author will be the viewpoint character.

3. Length: I recommend that this essay be at least 300 words long and no more than 550. Feel free to set your own word limits.

Some Advice:

1. This essay centers on the perceptions, thoughts, and wishes of the viewpoint character. Remember TIP #8: TFSS.

2. The success of this essay will depend, in substantial part, on the inclusion of a profusion of vivid sensory details.

They now write their essay. I recommend that you give them a minimum of 45 minutes for their writing. If they finish early, they revise and edit.

Post-Activity Review and Discussion

I recommend that, if you grade this work, you focus your assessment on creativity and on how they were able to build suspense and excitement over what didn't happen. Award the flow and coherence of their piece. Award how their piece reveals the heart and soul of the main character. Award how they weave what *doesn't* happen into their descriptions of what *does*.

Any follow-on discussion should center on these same attributes of this writing assignment.

Workout #23: Not My Voice

Quick Summary & Purpose

** **Purpose**: • Teach students to recognize the unique and defining elements of a writer's "voice" by mimicking a writer/character other than themselves.

Summary: This workout lets students intentionally shift the writer's voice of their own story into that of another known writer or clearly defined character. It is, I believe, the most effective way for students to understand the elements of, and limits of, voice.

Key Grades

Excellent for all grades.

Time Required

Part 1: 15 to 20 minutes
Part 2: Discussion: 15 minutes
Writing: 30 to 45 minutes
Sharing: 30 minutes

Introduction

There are many well-known writers, celebrities, and fiction characters that possess specific, unique, well-defined voices. Jane Austen, John Wayne, Shakespeare, a valley girl, a surfer dude, C3PO, a stuffy college professor, Marlon Brando, the waitress at a 1930s diner, etc. One excellent way to learn to control your own voice (as a writer)—as well as those of your character creations—is to mimic established voices in telling your story. That is the focus of this workout.

Directions

Part 1

Do not mention the theme of this workout, or anything about Part 2, to students until after their Part 1 writing has been completed. You don't want them to intentionally warp their initial writing to make their Part 2 work easier.

In Part 1, students write a short fiction story—topic of your choice. Target length is 150 to 250 words. Have them write this story and set it aside.

Part 2

Launch a class discussion about identifiable voices. Have students identify unique and famous voices (writers, celebrities, actors, fictional characters).

Start a list of their suggestions on the board. Have volunteers mimic each voice, and then have the class discuss what makes it distinct and memorable. Their answers should include (among other possible characteristics) word choice, word patterns, accent, vocabulary, repeated phrases, vocal qualities, and patterns. Which would be easy to mimic in writing? Which would be difficult?

The Writing Assignment for Part 2:

Assignment: *Rewrite the exact same story you wrote in Part 1 in one of the voices included on the class list.*

Students must tell the exact same story following the same progression of events.

Their goal is to make it sound as if it had actually been written by their chosen famous voice.

I recommend that you not provide examples for students to follow. Let them envision the voice and restructure the story.

However, as an example for teachers, let's take a story moment: the author meets someone of the opposite sex and is instantly smitten.

Here are examples of how three well-established voices might describe that moment.

Jane Austen:
Why, my dear reader, you can hardly imagine my embarrassment and the dizzying impropriety of the scandalous thoughts in my mind. I near to swooned and admit that I gasped at the fleeting sight of him rising to his fullest height. "Good sir, Modesty requires that I refrain from speaking my mind . . ."

John Wayne:
Why, shucks, ya' little missy. Darned if'n you ain't the pertiest thing I seen. Soon as I take care of them Injuns that are-a shootin' at us, I'll be back fer a kiss.

California Surfer:
So, dude. Like she's just standin' in the sand, almost as totally cool as a good curl at Doheny. I'd like go over to say like "hi," but my heart is pounding like I'm riding an 20 foot killer at Mavericks when it breaks left and you can shoot the curl almost 'till you'd like smash on the rocks. Ya' know, dude?

Encourage students to play with their revised story wording. This should be a fun exercise that holds a most valuable underpinning: developing the ability to write in a character's voice, not always in the author's.

Post-Activity Review and Discussion

Allow several students to share both versions of their story. Then focus the discussion on what was hard about throwing their story into another's voice.

Workout #24: Random Stories

Quick Summary & Purpose

** **Purpose:** • This is a fun, creative, energizing writing workout.

Summary: Students will have only a fixed amount of time to create a story that links four randomly selected pieces of story information.

Key Grades

Excellent for all grades.

Time Required

10 minutes to pick objects and to plan
15 minutes to write
15 minutes to share

Introduction

For many (if not most) students, the hardest part of writing is getting an idea for what to write about. It is always difficult to start a story when it can be about anything. Better to help students focus in on something—anything—specific. Get that initial idea, and it instantly sparks the images and events of the accompanying story. This workout is a fun way to get all students past those whiny, "I don't know what to write about . . ." blues and sparks their energy and eagerness to write.

Directions

Have two students each name a random object. (You have veto power if you think their choice is inappropriate). Keep it simple and reasonably generic (a ripped glove, a bent spoon, a deflated football, a cracked skateboard, etc.). Write these on the board. Have a third student pick a place (a story setting). Again, best to stay generic in their choice (a cave, the beach, a city park, a living room, a subway platform, the bottom of the ocean, etc.). Write this setting on the board.

A fourth student picks a weather condition (rain, sleet, hot sunshine, fog, etc.). This also goes on the board.

The final (fifth) student identifies a character by defining these four character traits: species, gender, age, and name. This information also goes on the board.

From *Writing Workouts to Develop Common Core Writing Skills: Step-by-Step Exercises, Activities, and Tips for Student Success, Grades 7–12* by Kendall Haven. Santa Barbara, CA: Libraries Unlimited. Copyright © 2015.

You want this workout to be valuable as well as fun. To do that, give students this writing assignment:

With those items identified, here is the writing assignment:

Assignment: *Write a story in 15 minutes that connects and incorporates these two objects, this setting, this weather condition, and this character.*

Before students begin to write, have them:

1. Create and define the main character (also their viewpoint character) for their story and create a goal and motive for that character.

2. Plan on making each of these five things the class pre-picked *important* to their story.

3. Make the story *exciting*! (Excitement comes from establishing risk and danger, not through action.)

Give students five minutes for planning and for jotting notes. Then 15 minutes to actually write.

Key goals for their writing are creativity and development of their main character and his/her story.

Post-Activity Review and Discussion

During follow-up discussions, have several students read their stories. Discuss by analyzing the Eight Essential Elements (see TIP #5, The Eight Essential Elements) and by assessing how able the students were in incorporating the assigned items as important parts of their story.

You'll find that both the writing and the reviewing are engaging and delightful to students.

Workout #25: *Por Qua* Stories

Quick Summary & Purpose

** **Purpose:** • Learn to weave factual information into strong, character-based story development and writing.

Summary: This is a different format for a research-written report. The idea is to provide greater motive for student research efforts, and to make the writing much more fun. This is a way to blend the fun and writing control of fiction with factual research.

Key Grades

Excellent for all grades

Time Required

Rather than being a separate activity, assigning *por qua* stories is part of existing student research, study, and writing work. No extra time is required. However, most teachers create (and students eagerly want) specific blocks of time at the end for students to share their creations.

Introduction

This activity is designed to be used as part of a factual curriculum research effort (typically either for science or history class—but certainly not limited to those two). I have seen classes create wonderful *por qua* stories after studying aspects of space, geography, the environment, American history, etc.

"*Por qua*" literally translates as "for why." *Por qua* stories explain why things are as they are. Many of Rudyard Kipling's stories serve as *por qua* stories. So do many of the stories from Native American cultures.

Por qua stories are fun. They provide fictional characters and fictional events to explain why things are as we currently find them to be: why the beaver has a flat tail, why the planets circle the sun, why the skunk has a white stripe, why there are tides in the ocean, why the ocean is salty, why the land is shaped as it is, why rivers run to the sea. Any possible "why" question can be answered by a *por qua*–formatted story.

Por qua stories are good choices for student writing because they feature simple, easy story structures. The main character has a flaw or a discontent that causes him/her to upset the "normal" status quo. All the characters around this main character react—generally quite negatively. Conflicts, problems, and struggles ensue. Things end up with a new "normal"—what we experience today.

From *Writing Workouts to Develop Common Core Writing Skills: Step-by-Step Exercises, Activities, and Tips for Student Success, Grades 7–12* by Kendall Haven. Santa Barbara, CA: Libraries Unlimited. Copyright © 2015.

This structure gives students a chance to let their imaginations fly! It also forces them to develop and rely on character elements more than plotting—an excellent writing habit to develop for all forms and genres of writing.

And those stories are always fun! Fun to read and fun to write. The idea of this exercise is to use the fun and enjoyment of a *por qua* format to let students research and explain actual natural phenomena.

Directions

Read several *por qua* stories that explain phenomena within the general subject that your class is studying. Discuss the form, character development, and plotting patterns.

As the class studies some unit for which they will write a *por qua* story, have each student pick one specific subject-related phenomenon he or she wants to write about. This should come to you for your approval in the form:

"I will explain why the _____ came to be (or is as we now see it)."

Make sure that each chosen phenomenon is sufficiently specific so that it will be easy to write about and also will allow the student to incorporate significant study and research information.

After you approve the topic, students need to create the characters, goals, motives, problems, and struggles of their story. All *por qua* stories end with the physical reality we actually see around us. Use the *Por Qua* Story Planning Sheet (next page) or design your own. Completing this type of form forces students to plan their story before they begin to write.

Once you approve their planning sheet, students are turned loose to write their stories. While writing, they may not violate known factual information—known science or history. Rather, successful *por qua* stories use as much factual information as possible in weaving their fictional explanations.

Por Qua ("For Why?") Story Planning Sheet

Title:

Phenomenon I will explain: Why the _____ came to be the way it is today.

How things are at the Beginning:

How things are at the End:

My Main Character:

Key Flaw (What gets this character in trouble):

Other interesting character traits I'll use for this character:

How "normal" is disturbed:

Other central characters (and their defining characteristics):

Key story events:

Post-Activity Review and Discussion

This is an excellent writing assignment for the inclusion of a formal revision step. When they turn in their papers, don't worry about spelling, grammar, and punctuation. Not yet. First revise. Does the story make sense? Do the characters seem interesting, and do their actions explain the phenomenon supposedly being explained? Is there a climax moment/scene in the story? Do you clearly see main character goals and motives? How can you suggest ways to make the story more fun and clever?

Now let students take those notes and revise. I like to give these notes and ideas to students in live, one-on-one discussions rather than as written notes.

Collect the revised papers and now conduct a line-editing review. This is the time for spelling, grammar, etc. checks and corrections. Be sure to tell students what each of these steps is for and why you are separating revision from editing. (There is no need to check spelling in paragraphs that will be rewritten (or cut) during revision. Once students edit, they tend to be far less willing to revise.)

Finally, let students share their work. Use their stories to launch a discussion about what elements create fun, captivating, interesting *por qua* stories

Workout #26: Perfect Birthdays

Quick Summary & Purpose

** **Purpose**: • Dramatically demonstrate the necessity of conflict and problems (and their associated Risk & Danger) to writing effectiveness and success.

Summary: This workout asks students to describe a perfect day. It always sounds fun at the outset. However, the writing becomes instantly mired in the perfection of the day. Things that go smoothly and without problems make for boring writing. The challenge of this workout is to incorporate these essential narrative elements into a story based on everything going right.

Key Grades

Excellent for all grades

Time Required

Step 1: 10 minutes
Step 2: 10 to 15 minutes
Step 3: 20 to 30 minutes
Step 4: 30 to 45 minutes
Post Activity Discussion: 15 to 20 minutes

Introduction

It's always easy to write about great conflicts and struggles. But what do you write when nothing goes wrong? That is a much greater challenge for writers. Yet it is an important ability to develop. How do you make the written piece engaging and attention-grabbing when some of the most powerful writing tools (conflict and problem, risk and danger, struggles) are seemingly unavailable? That is the exact situation students find themselves in when they try to describe a perfect day—one in which, presumably, nothing goes wrong.

Directions

Step 1

Give students this writing assignment and let them write on it for 10 minutes. Hold any question about the assignment to a minimum.

Assignment: *Describe what would be your perfect birthday.*

Step 2

Now evaluate and discuss the writing. Was it hard to write? Did students quickly run out of things to write? Why? (*No conflict or problems; no story!*) Are the descriptions by other students boring to hear? Why? Discuss what creates suspense (*goal and motive and obstacles*) and excitement (*risk and danger created by problems and conflicts*) in a story. Why are those absent in this descriptive piece? How can student writers reinsert them into this piece? (*through the thoughts and feelings of the main character, through that character's fears and worries*)

Step 3

After this discussion, students should outline the key elements of the Eight Essential Elements (see below). This can either be done with each student working alone, with students working in pairs, or with students individually developing this information followed by a chance to share and revise with a partner.

They need to define:

- **Main Character:** Themselves. This is all about *their* perception of the perfect birthday.
- **Character traits:** Think of two traits about yourself (even quirks, fears, flaws, or habits) that will seem endearing or positive from the viewpoint of the reader; that will make readers empathize with you and your efforts to seek a perfect birthday.
- **Goal:** List the one thing that would make it a perfect birthday and then up to four other slightly less important things that would happen as part of this perfect birthday.
- **Motives:** Why do you want (especially) the primary goal you stated above? Make sure that at least one of these motives will be considered to be a noble motive by the reader—instead of all being selfish ("Gimme, gimme, gimme whatever *I* want!")
- **Problems & conflict; risk & danger.** What could go wrong? How likely is it to happen? How worried are you that it will go wrong?

Step 4

Now rewrite the descriptive essay incorporating this information into it. Give students 20 to 30 minutes for this descriptive writing.

Post-Activity Review and Discussion

Compare the two versions of this essay. Allow several students to read both versions. Discuss the differences and their effect on the reader (or listener).

Emphasize the need for planning (create first; write second) and for considering all of the Eight Essential Elements. Also note how easily we are lured away from methodically and careful planning by the rush of the first idea that leaps into our minds. Don't forget or ignore that idea. But don't let it take over your mind and thought, either.

Workout #27: Your Scene

Quick Summary & Purpose

** **Purpose:** • Develop a feel for creating one individual scene (one event) in a longer story while being consistent with the voice of the author and the defined nature of all story characters.

Summary: Assuming that students have become intimately familiar with a story, its structure, and its characters, they will be in position to create an event of their own to insert into the plotting sequence of that story.

Key Grades

Excellent for all grades

Time Required

20 to 40 minutes for writing
Extra for any rounds of revision and self- or peer-editing you want to include.

Introduction

Many stories—even novels—represent a sequence—a linear progression—of individual events. Event A happens, leaving the main character in position B. The character then attempts event C . . . and so forth. This workout fits best into stories where a character makes repeated attempts to accomplish the same objective all (or most) of which fail.

The needed pattern is: A character has a defined goal and attempts action A to achieve it, but fails, leaving him/him exactly where he started. The character then tries action B, which also fails and leaves him back where he started. And so forth.

Directions

Find a story that includes the plotting pattern described above and read it with your class. A classic cartoon example of this plotting pattern is the series of Road Runner/Wile E. Coyote cartoons in which Wile E. repeatedly tries and fails to catch the Road Runner. Many folk tales are written in this format and plotting pattern. A character struggles through three or four unsuccessful attempts to reach a goal before she ever devises a plan that will succeed.

Share the story with your class and then make this assignment:

Assignment: *Write one attempt by that character to achieve this same goal.*

Each student's contribution must:

1. Begin with the main character in that same physical starting position already established in the story.

2. Use the voice and all character traits of the main character and of all side characters that have been developed in the original story.

3. Use the conflicts (antagonists) and risks and dangers previously established in the story.

4. Create and describe a new plan (scheme) for the main character to try in that character's continuing attempt to achieve his/her goal.

5. Use known traits of the main character (or reveal new traits for the main character) that will unravel this new plan and get that character into (and then barely back out of) BIG TROUBLE.

6. End with the main character back exactly where he or she started, having failed in this additional attempt to achieve his or her goal.

Rather than being restrictive for student creativity, these structural mandates allow students to focus on the details and specifics of the events of their story and free them to focus their attention on the character interactions and reactions.

Emphasize for your students that their focus while writing should be on the: Details, details, details—especially on TFFS (see TIP #8). Show us how each character thinks, feels, and reacts to each situation and development.

Post-Activity Review and Discussion

Allow students to share the events they have created. Start a class discussion through which you try to collectively identify what makes a new attempt in an established pattern fun, exciting, and engaging. What creates excitement? What increases suspense in the story? Which were more fun to listen to: plans that seemed plausible or ones that seemed a bit outrageous and instantly doomed to failure? Was it fun to figure out in advance exactly how and why the plan would fail? (In writing terms, that is one form of foreshadowing—signaling the reader about what to anticipate in the story's future.)

Workout #28: Inferring a Character

Quick Summary & Purpose

** **Purpose:** • Students will become more consciously aware of how, and to what extent, they subconsciously and automatically make a number of character inferences form scant story information. This is a critical awareness for effective narrative writing.

Summary: We all love to watch—and to laugh at—classic cartoons. However, all cartoons are strongly character based. They provide the perfect opportunity to explore how alluring characters are created and presented.

Key Grades

Excellent for all grades.

Time Required

45 minutes total

Introduction

Cartoons (especially the "Saturday morning classics") are always a delight to watch and to laugh at. They are also powerful character studies. It is that aspect of a cartoon that you will use in this workout to make your students more aware of the tools available to them—as writers—to develop and present their fiction and nonfiction characters.

Directions

Many of the old classic cartoons are available for free download on the Internet. My favorite for this workout are the Road Runner cartoons. My second favorite are Bugs Bunny cartoons that pit Bugs against Elmer Fudd.

Download a cartoon (let's assume you pick one of the Road Runner episodes) to your laptop and use the computer projection system in your classroom to play the cartoon for your students.

They will certainly be engaged and pay attention.

In this cartoon there are two characters (the Road Runner and Wile E. Coyote, or Bugs and Elmer). Pick the villain to analyze during this workout.

Let students work in teams of two. They are to list everything they know and can infer from this cartoon about this character. I usually give them 15 minutes for this task.

From *Writing Workouts to Develop Common Core Writing Skills: Step-by-Step Exercises, Activities, and Tips for Student Success, Grades 7–12* by Kendall Haven. Santa Barbara, CA: Libraries Unlimited. Copyright © 2015.

As prompts, ask (or write on the board) the following areas for them to consider:

- Personality
- Physical abilities
- Mental abilities
- Dreams and goals
- Fears
- Flaws and disabilities
- Natural talents
- Strengths and weaknesses
- What I like about this character
- What I dislike about this character.

Post-Activity Review and Discussion

Have individual teams read their lists. Discuss and refine as a class as you build a master list on the board. Once a good master list of character traits exists on the board, redirect the discussion to this question:

How did you decide that (the character) exhibits this trait?

That question takes students back to the source material. As they tear apart the original, they will uncover techniques that they each can use to increase the allure and appeal of their own characters.

Workout #29: Scene Game

Quick Summary & Purpose

** **Purpose**: • Clearly demonstrate the value of improved scenic visualization and detail prior to writing.

Summary: Students tend not to adequately visualize the places (settings) where their stories and other narratives take place before they begin to write. This workout both makes them aware of this common failing and gives them a powerful corrective tool they can use with peers and friends anytime they plan a narrative.

Key Grades

Excellent for all grades.

Time Required

20 to 25 minutes per use

Introduction

We rarely take the time to really visualize each scene of our story. Until a student gets into the habit of creating expansive, detailed mental images of each scene and character, it's nice to get some help in the process from other students.

Directions

This is an exercise to use just before actual writing work begins on a story or essay. Students should already have the story idea in mind, should have developed the story's characters, the ending point, and the general plot sequencing.

Divide the class into groups of five. A six-person group will do, but more is unwieldy. A four-person group is passable, but fewer won't generate the needed barrage of ideas.

The groups sit in chairs in a circle. One student at a time is chosen to be "it." When it is their turn, that student gets 45 seconds to describe to the group an important scene in the story he or she is going to write. This description should mention who is present and generally what happens, but should concentrate on a description of the setting, the physical scene, itself.

The group now has two minutes to ask any question about that physical setting. The group act like suspicious police officers grilling a suspect. No question is too detailed or trivial. Their goal is to either catch this student in a contradiction in the information he or she provides or to ask questions that momentarily stump the writer, that cause that student to think of aspects of the scene he or she had never thought of before.

The writer who is "it" *must* answer every question. The writer may not answer, "I don't know," or "It doesn't matter." He must answer the question even if it means he has to make up an answer on the spot. He, of course, isn't committed to that answer and may change it later as he writes. But having to answer will expand his image of each story scene.

The groups should be encouraged to explore all five senses during this questioning and to search for possible inconsistencies or gaps in the writer's story.

After two minutes of being peppered by the group's questions, that student shifts off the hot seat and a second student moves on.

You should drift among the groups as you time each questioning period. Look for groups that are struggling to invent tough, probing questions, or where the group has floundered, unable to think of what to ask. Help them by interjecting one or two obscure questions about background sounds, where the shadows fall, what color the curtains are, and whether there is any dust on them, how humid it is, or some such thing. That modeling will encourage them to follow suit with more effective and beneficial questions of their own.

Variation: The Character Game

The same game in the same group structure can be used to develop students' image of their main characters and of the level of detail they hold for those characters.

The pattern and time allocations remain the same. However, when a student is "it," she describes her main character (instead of a physical setting). Each student's goal is to paint as interesting and complete an image of this character as possible in the allotted time.

If your students would be helped by a bit of informational prompting, here are six questions I often provide. These questions both help students decide what to say about their character and stimulate better questions from the group.

1. What are the goals, flaws, problems, risks, and dangers this character faces in this story?

2. What are the unique and interesting aspects of this character's physical being and personality? What are their hopes and fears?

3. How does this character want the story to end, and why?

4. How does this character feel about the story's antagonist, and why?

5. Why does the writer like this character?

6. Why does the writer think we should care about this character? What will make the character interesting and unique to a reader?

The group now has two minutes to ask questions about this character, or about any of the statements the student made during the introduction. The group's goal in asking these questions is two-fold. First, they should clear up anything that isn't clear to them about this character. If it isn't clear to them, it probably isn't clear to the writer, and won't be clear to a reader. Second, they should probe for any undefined or ambiguous aspects of this character in the writer's mind.

Again, if you want to offer prompts to students, here is the list I use.

- Questions about any aspect of the character are legitimate and valuable.
- "Where was this character born?"
- "What are this character's favorite and least favorite foods?"
- "What color are their eyes?"
- "What was this character's favorite thing to do when he was half his present age?"
- "Name three things this character is afraid of,"
- "What sports is this character good at and bad at,"
- "Does the character like to comb her hair?"
- "How many friends does this character have, and why?"
- And so on, and so on. All character questions are fair game.

The student who is "it" must answer all questions, even if he or she has to make up an answer on the spot. But the student should be encouraged to ask the group for ideas and opinions on any aspect of the character he or she is uncertain about. This is an opportunity for the writer to seek peer ideas and help in developing and defining the character.

After a two-minute question and discussion period, the group selects the next student to be "it."

Post-Activity Review and Discussion

Writers never think of all the aspects of a scene. It is valuable to have others help widen the writer's horizon and make him think about aspects of a scene and a story he hadn't considered. Every writer needs this help. The tougher the questions the group asks, the more help it is for the writer.

During this exercise, all group members benefit from each question—even if they weren't on the hot seat. They still consider the answers to every question as if it had been asked about their own story.

After this exercise, do your students see the scenes of their stories better? Do they see them in more detail? Do they see them more clearly? More detail means the story will be easier to write and will seem more real to the reader.

The same concepts apply to the characters we write about—both real and fictional characters. Successful writing depends on creating more complete and more detailed images of each major story character. Strong images include not only the present physical look and circumstances of a character, but also the character's history, memories, attitudes, beliefs, and mannerisms. Groups help us expand our creative processes and produce stronger, richer, more interesting characters.

Workout #30: Cause and Effect

Quick Summary & Purpose

** **Purpose**: • Make the concept of cause and effect a conscious and useful writing tool for students.

Summary: Almost all cultures believe in cause and effect. A past action causes a current situation. A current action will cause some future situation. Virtually all students use cause-and-effect thinking as they write. However, most do it automatically, subconsciously. This workout brings that concept up front and center as a conscious planning tool for their writing.

Key Grades

Good for all grades

Time Required

Oral Exercise: 15 minutes
Written Exercise: 15-20 minutes

Introduction

Everyone tries to figure out a story as they read it. But how do they do that? They assume that the law of cause and effect is operating in this story. That's how. They assume that the information and actions early on in the story are the causes that set into motion consequences that appear later in the story. John lies near the beginning of a story. Readers know he's going to regret it and get in trouble later. Cause and effect. Student writers often forget this most basic story structure while they are writing. They simply have things "happen." This exercise is designed to remind them of the power and flow of cause and effect.

Nothing is more basic in both eastern and western philosophies than the idea of cause and effect, or karma. One thing leads to another. Actions today cause events tomorrow. What you sow today, so shall you reap tomorrow. It is a powerful and reliable story structure to use in writing exercises.

Directions

This workout should first be demonstrated to the whole class, and may then be performed by smaller groups of three or four. Briefly discuss "cause and effect" with your students to make sure that they correctly understand the terms and the concept.

From *Writing Workouts to Develop Common Core Writing Skills: Step-by-Step Exercises, Activities, and Tips for Student Success, Grades 7–12* by Kendall Haven.

112   Santa Barbara, CA: Libraries Unlimited. Copyright © 2015.

The exercise starts with one student inventing and describing a fictional event. They tell about something that happened. They *do not* explain *why* it happened. They just make up and tell *what* happened.

Student #1: "A cat wandered, howling, down an alley."

Student #2 now invents and tells *why* that event happened. That is, #2 defines the specific actions in the past caused this action (the "effect") to happen in the story's present.

Student #2: "The cat was howling because it was lost and hadn't eaten in six days. On a family vacation it had jumped out of the arms of the girl who owned it. The family couldn't find the cat and had to leave for home without it."

If the class isn't satisfied with, or isn't sure of, this causal relationship, have #2 explain and justify it. If necessary, amend #2's event so that the class understands the cause-and-effect relationship between the events provided by #1 and #2. This is an important part of the exercise. The class must ensure that everyone can see and accept the cause-effect relationship between these two events.

It is always surprising to see how much more interest is created in student #1's event after student #2 has provided its causal background. At this point you may pause to discuss the direct cause-and-effect relationship in this story and how it defines the necessary plot line of the story.

Now student #3 makes up why the situation and events described by #2 came to be. That is, student #3 invents a cause for the actions described by #2 that were made up to be a cause for the action described by #1.

Student #3: "The family loved their cat, Scooter. But they knew Scooter would never survive on her own while they left for a three-week driving vacation. Scooter was scared of everything and needed lots of love and attention. They decided to take Scooter with them on the car trip."

Every cause leads to an action or event that becomes the root cause for the next action. Every action has a root cause lying somewhere in the past. Again, the class must come to agreement that #3's description forms a plausible cause for #2's action.

Now go forward. Student #4 creates the next event in the story that follows after, and because of, the original event described by #1.

Student #4: "A man threw a shoe at Scooter and yelled at her to be quiet. Scooter collapsed, trembling with hunger and fear behind a slimy dumpster where she met a cockroach."

Again the class debates and approves #4's description. Finally, student #5 creates yet another event that flows after and because of the event described by #4.

Student #5: "Scooter found that the cockroach was part of a large, friendly family. Scooter moved in with the cockroaches (even though her room was much too small) and lived happily ever after."

A string of five causes and effects has been laid out. Do they define a story? From them could your students track back to the core character information that defines a story? Can the class members see how this whole flow of cause and effect leads from step to step? Is event #5 more interesting because you know its causal background of events #1 through #4? Does event #5 tend to resolve the situation (or problem) naturally created in event #1?

Written Exercise

A fun way to have students think about cause-and-effect sequencing as they write is to write a progressive story. Each student begins a story. The stories are then progressively passed around the room so that each story receives contributions from five students.

The rules:

1. Begin your story about 2/3rds of the way down the front side of a piece of 8.5 X 11 paper.

2. Each person writes for 30 seconds.

3. During this initial 30-second block, each student must identify a character, the situation they are in, and an action they are currently doing.

They all now write for 30 seconds and pass their paper to someone else.

4. This second person reads what has been written and decides what event in the immediate past caused (created) this situation for this character.

5. They write this scene just above the initial entry (starting about 1/3rd of the way down the page).

They will write for 30 seconds and pass the paper on to a new contributor.

6. This 3rd contributor to each of the stories decides what event (previous to that described by the 2nd contributor) caused *that* event to happen.

7. They will write this scene beginning at the top of the page.

They will write for 30 seconds and pass the paper on to a new contributor.

8. The 4th contributor will decide what near future event is the result of (caused by) the original scene (the bottom of side 1).

9. They will write this scene beginning at the top of the back side of the page.

They will write for 30 seconds and pass the paper on to a new contributor.

10. The 5th and final contributor will decide what future event is the result of (caused by) the previous four scenes.

11. They will write this scene on the back side of the page below that scene contributed by student #4.

Collect the papers and scan to make sure that students used logical cause-and-effect thinking in their design of each of their contributions. If many of the jumps between scenes are illogical, or do not fully explain the cause-and-effect relationship between adjacent scenes, discuss with the class and repeat the workout.

Post-Activity Review and Discussion

Every reader expects story events to flow logically from one scene to the next. Readers often can't *anticipate* the exact nature of this flow, but should be able to see it as logical, if not inevitable, in *hindsight*. As a writer lays out the scenes of a story, he or she can use this concept to first plan, and later review and edit, the sequencing of scenes the writer has created.

If the story seems to drift without powerful tension and purpose, one way to repair it is to check scenes that lead up to any dull, aimless spots and make sure causal actions are laid down in these scenes that must come to fruition during the present scene. The causal action is like hearing one shoe hit the floor. Readers can't put the story down until they've heard the other shoe fall. That is, until they have heard the resultant effect scene.

OTHER BOOKS OF WRITING ACTIVITIES AND GAMES

These are a few of the many good sources of writing and story muscle-building games and workouts.

Haven, Kendall. *Story Smart: Using the Science of Story to Persuade, Inspire, Influence, and Teach.* Santa Barbara, CA: Libraries Unlimited, 2014.

Haven, Kendall. *Story Proof: The Science Behind the Startling Power of Story.* Westport, CT: Libraries Unlimited, 2009.

Haven, Kendall. *Get It Write! Creating Lifelong Writers from Expository to Narrative.* Portsmouth, NH: Teacher Ideas Press, 2004.

Haven, Kendall. *Super Simple Storytelling.* Englewood, CO: Teacher Ideas Press, 2000.

Haven, Kendall. *Write Right: Creative Writing Using Storytelling Techniques.* Englewood, CO: Teacher Ideas Press, 1999.

INDEX

ABOUT THE AUTHOR

KENDALL HAVEN is a master storyteller and author of 34 books who has conducted writing workshops at over 1,600 schools and has performed for total audiences of over 6.5 million. His published works include 24 books from Libraries Unlimited, including *Story Proof: The Science Behind the Startling Power of Story*; *Get It Write! Creating Lifelong Writers from Expository to Narrative*; and *Write Right! Creative Writing Using Storytelling Techniques*.